"A fascinating excursion into Foucault's thought in the late 1970s, in which Japan is an 'enigma' that works to clarify his own thoughts. In his presentations to Japanese audiences, the reader overhears Foucault explaining his thinking to himself in an engaging and often personal manner".

Carol Gluck, George Sansom Professor of History, Columbia University.

" 'The end of the era of Western philosophy'. Foucault was often less guarded abroad and would drop gems in conversation with foreign scholars that he might not have shared in France. These brilliant Japan Lectures are a case in point. In a wide-ranging set of talks delivered in Japan in 1978 – ranging over topics from sexuality, to discipline, to power, knowledge, and philosophy– Foucault revealed himself and his ongoing thought processes. Expertly edited by John Rajchman and beautifully translated, these Japan Lectures offer a new window into his work".

Bernard E. Harcourt is a chaired professor at Columbia University and the École des hautes études en sciences sociales in Paris and has edited a range of works by Foucault in French and English, including the Gallimard Pléaide edition of Surveiller et punir.

"A fascinating rediscovery of Foucault in Asia. *The Japan Lectures* presents an exclusive collection of the French philosopher's lectures, interviews, and conversations during his trips to postwar Japan, available for the first time in English translation. This book transforms our understanding of Foucault and his reflections on the limits of Western thought by posing a fundamental question: Will the philosophy of the future emerge outside Europe?"

Lydia H. Liu, Wun Tsun Tam Professor in the Humanities, Columbia University, author of The Freudian Robot.

The Japan Lectures

This book makes available, for the first time in English, lectures and interviews that Foucault gave in Japan in 1978, reconstructing their context, and isolating the question of their singular relevance for us today. In these forgotten lectures, in a free and often informal style, Foucault explores, together with his Japanese interlocutors, what it would mean to take up, from outside Europe, the questions he was raising at the time about Revolution and Enlightenment in the traditions of European critical thought. In a series of wide-ranging discussions, on sexuality and its history, non-Christian forms of spirituality, new forms of political movements, and the role of knowledge, power, and truth in them, Foucault examines these questions in relationship to Asia. He had hoped these questions, very much debated at the time in postwar Japan, would be the start of new forms of translation, publication, and exchange. At the heart of the lectures is thus a search for the creation of a new sort of transnational collaboration, recasting the history of European colonialism and opening to a philosophy no longer simply Western, yet to come.

The Japan Lectures thus contribute to the new scholarship in Asian and in translation studies which has long since moved away from earlier "Area Studies"; at the same time, it participates in the new scholarship about Foucault's own work and itinerary, following the publication of an extraordinary wealth of materials left unfinished or unpublished by his untimely death. In these ways, *The Japan Lectures* help us to better see the implications of Foucault's work for philosophy in the 21st century.

Michel Foucault was one of the greatest philosophers and intellectuals of the 20th century.

John Rajchman, presenter and author of the introduction, is a philosopher and a professor in the Department of Art History and Archaeology at Columbia University. He has written extensively on Foucault, and more generally on postwar French philosophy.

Michel
Foucault

The Japan Lectures
A Transnational Critical Encounter

Presented and introduced by **John Rajchman**

Routledge
Taylor & Francis Group
LONDON AND NEW YORK

First published 2024
by Routledge
4 Park Square, Milton Park, Abingdon, Oxon OX14 4RN

and by Routledge
605 Third Avenue, New York, NY 10158

Routledge is an imprint of the Taylor & Francis Group, an informa business

British Library Cataloguing-in-Publication Data
A catalogue record for this book is available from the British Library

ISBN: 978-1-032-28605-1 (hbk)
ISBN: 978-1-032-30174-7 (pbk)
ISBN: 978-1-003-30376-3 (ebk)

DOI: 10.4324/9781003303763

Typeset in Joanna
by Deanta Global Publishing Services, Chennai, India

For Daniel Defert, without whom none of this would have been possible

Contents

ACKNOWLEDGMENTS

This book would not have been possible without the invaluable contributions of many people.

First and foremost, I'd like to thank Daniel Defert, who accompanied Foucault during the Japan Lectures, for his ongoing support for the project from the outset, and for our many extraordinary conversations in the process.

I'd like to thank Lydia Liu and Bernard Faure of Columbia University for our many enlightening discussions of the project from the start; Yuma Terada for his steadfast commitment in its realization; and Shiguéhiko Hasumi, for his willingness to take part and his remarkable interview.

I'd like to thank the expert and congenial team of translators for their tireless dedication to the project: Peter Conor, Emily Sun, Anne Boyman, Alexia Trigo, Zineb Belghiti, Alice Mahoney, and, in particular, Anne Boyman for assembling and working with the team and for her assistance throughout.

In addition, many thanks to Carolina Sprovieri for her research on the materials kept at IMEC about Foucault's time in Japan; to Mia Xing for her work in preparing the final manuscript; to Michelle Chu for her early assistance with the project; and to Tracy Jiao, for her invaluable help with the production of the book.

FOUCAULT IN ASIA

An Introduction

At the start of 1978, Michel Foucault went on an extended trip to Japan, accompanied by Daniel Defert. He gave a number of interviews and lectures about his work, carried on a series of discussions with Japanese intellectuals in public and private, visited prisons unlike those he had studied in Europe, joined a demonstration at an airport on a trip organized by the French Embassy. Some of the resulting lectures and discussions were published at the time in Japanese in various journals. They appear here for the first time in a new English-language translation in a much-altered world. We can now see they encapsulate a key moment in Foucault's thought and his itinerary, involving an unrealized project, which would stay with him until his untimely death six years later—a multiple experiment in a new sort of transnational critical thought.

The Japan Lectures include both *dits* and *écrits*, sayings and writings, in which, in open discussion with his Japanese interlocutors, Foucault presented the new questions he was exploring in his own work and imagined new ways of developing them in places outside Europe, as he had done earlier in Brazil, Tunisia, and the United States, but in this case without the benefit of a language "in common". Conducted in French, with Japanese translation, and an occasional use of English with interlocutors who didn't know French, the Lectures involved an exchange that Foucault hoped to bring back with him to Paris. Not anchored in any one publication in France before or after, spread out instead

DOI: 10.4324/9781003303763-1

in a kind of multiple conversation, going off in different directions, generating new ideas and historical hypotheses, the Lectures can now be seen as a kind of time capsule of a singular moment in Foucault's thought. What then is the hinge which links this earlier moment to our own? It is perhaps to be found in the search for a new way of doing critical philosophy, then itself in a moment of crisis, captured in this striking remark, in a conversation with Zen monks, on the eve of his departure:

> European thought finds itself at a turning point. This turning point, on the historical level, is nothing other than the end of imperialism ... There is no philosopher who marks this epoch. For it is the end of the era of Western philosophy. Thus, if a philosophy of the future exists, it must be born outside of Europe or it must be born of encounters and reverberations between Europe and non-Europe.[1]

Returning to Paris, in a lecture at the French Philosophical Society entitled "What is Critique?", Foucault would take up these questions again in a more European context, raising them later that year in turn in a fraught moment of Revolution in Iran, then the following year in a remarkable lecture about "political rationality" at Stanford University.[2] In all three cases, Foucault elaborated questions which earlier had run throughout the Japan Lectures and the search, in a Japanese context, for a new kind of critical philosophy, conducted in many places and national languages at once, cutting across the imagined boundaries that separate them.

A philosophy of the future then—if there is to be one—can no longer be based on a "master thinker" in any one country or language or in any monolithic narrative with fixed starting and endpoints. On the contrary, it will require many languages, places, and civilizations at once, brought together not by a higher truth or a supervenient method, but instead by a constant agitation, ever renewed, punctuated by unpredictable "events", that force us to rethink the past together and imagine other possibilities in the present. Why was the end of European imperialism and of the great anti-imperialist responses to it, the critical event through which such questions were then being posed to us? What does that mean for the very idea of "Western" and therefore for "non-Western" philosophy? Through what kinds of exchange, what sorts of public spaces, and the related function of political intellectuals can we invent new forms of thinking critically together? In the Japan Lectures, Foucault was quietly exploring all these questions.

For many years the Lectures would remain in Japanese in various publications. It is unlikely Foucault himself ever imagined they would have a life outside of them. Things would change only in 1994, with a four-volume publication of Foucault's "writings and sayings", a part of the larger publication of Foucault's Courses at the Collège de France, as well as a wealth of additional material, which now completely dwarfs the publication of Foucault's work in French at the time of his death, changing, in the process, our sense of their nature and their legacy.

Deleuze already had a keen sense that this material would transform our understanding of Foucault's work and its legacy, allowing us to see his interviews as an integral part of his work, but starting with the actual publication of *Dits et écrits*, this idea would acquire a new, transnational sense. For each of his great historical studies, published in France and in French, Deleuze thought, in his interviews and related works, Foucault would imagine other possibilities, in an ongoing process of "becoming-other".[3] But after 1976, there in fact would be no such book in French to anchor Foucault's thought; everything would become part of "writings and sayings", spread out in many languages, today supplemented by the Courses and additional materials.

The Japan Lectures, given in 1978, two years later, are a case in point. Daniel Defert, very much Foucault's partner in the Japan trip, would also play a key role in the ongoing publication and translation of this extraordinary *Nachlass* and the new questions and the new uses that it would open up. A key aim of the publication of *Dits et écrits* in 1994 from which the Japan Lectures are taken was in particular to show how much Foucault's work had been "transnational" from the start, carried on in many places outside France, and, as in the case of these Lectures, outside Europe. Foucault in fact had spent as much time outside as inside France, and in those foreign places, he increasingly found ways of becoming "foreign" to the French world in which he had grown up. He would later say as much himself in a late interview with Steven Riggens, in which he declares: "I suffer and still suffer from certain aspects of French social and political life. That's the reason I left France in 1955".[4] One aim of the collection and translation of the materials in *Dits et écrits* was then to make this foreign activity available for the first time in French. The publication, carefully specifying the places and circumstances of each of the "sayings and writings", was accompanied by a remarkable Chronology, drawn up by Daniel Defert, which would allow one to see those times and places as part of an ongoing voyage of sorts, thus upending any attempt to find in Foucault's biography a secret that might explain his work. Rather it would become possible to read Foucault's work as an ongoing itinerary of constant displacement and rethinking, much in the spirit in which Foucault himself would declare that all his works were "fragments of autobiography". In contrast to other languages, notably Japanese and Brazilian, this entire endeavor would be ignored in English, where the Chronology was eliminated, and translations made from selected materials, often given new titles, geared to suit the preoccupations of American universities. None of the Japan Lectures would be retained in this operation. Not only were the Lectures lost in the process, but also any sense of their role in Foucault's ongoing political itinerary. While American universities would continue to play a key role in the dissemination of "French Theory" throughout the world, that role would itself change, particularly in relation to the questions about European colonialism Foucault was raising in the Japan Lectures.

Perhaps no one national language is ever sufficient for such transnational critical activity, and in any case, from early on, Foucault's own work involved many, as with the several languages involved in the publication and subsequent translations of the Japan Lectures themselves. The belated translation of the Japan Lectures into English in this volume is no exception, even if it now involves a more "global" English, including many for whom English is a second language, no longer dominated in the same way by American English alone. In an extraordinary way, it is in just such terms that many years later the Japan Lectures would be rediscovered by a new group of scholars, working at once across several different languages, with a common focus on the impact of colonialism, and on the ways Japan and Asia had been studied and their "modern history" told. Taking off from a collaborative essay in 2006 by Jon Solomon and Nicolai Sakai, entitled "Translation, Biopolitics, Colonial Differences", this new approach drew on a transformation in the critical study of Asia, no longer hostage to postwar area studies, instead engaging new critical histories of colonialism, themselves no longer simply "anti-" or "post-", involving instead the multiple temporalities of hybrid or mixed forms of translation and reinvention. Republished in a number of ways and contexts—in 2022, in relation to "The End of Pax Americana"—this initiative helped introduce a new framework, bringing together traveling theory, de-colonial critique, and the politics of translation, all in a search for a new sort of transnational citizenship, of which Foucault's lectures in Japan in 1978 then appeared as a remarkable anticipation.[5] In particular, this rediscovery of the Lectures helped underscore the role that "travel" and "theory" had played in them, and in their eventual publication and translation, as Sandro Mezzadra would already argue in 2011, in a striking essay, itself translated from the Italian, entitled "En voyage: Foucault et la critique postcoloniale".[6] Expanding on what Edward Said had already called "traveling theory", Mezzadra raised the question of the sense in which travel had been an integral part of Foucault's critical project, not simply in his own itinerary, but also in the larger historical and political forces driving the way critical theory itself travels and is taken up or reinvented elsewhere. The two processes would come together in 1978, at a critical moment in the wake of European imperialism, at once in Japan and France, or more generally, Asia and Europe. Thus, on the one hand, travel becomes a critical or theoretical matter only when it offers a way of setting aside one's own "discourse", one's preconceptions, offering instead a way of becoming "foreign to oneself" in a new kind of exchange with others—at once personal and political—as, for example, earlier, in the 1930s, with Walter Benjamin's Moscow Diary. On the other hand, "critical theory" itself travels only when transported through larger historical and political forces, like those, precisely, of the forces of European colonialism in the 19th and 20th centuries and the anti-imperialist opposition to them, which would spread European critical thought throughout the world, setting up, in the process, discursive conditions in which philosophy or theory would be translated and reinvented outside Europe. It is in this sense, to use Solomon and Sakai's terms, that there is a "politics of translation", beyond the simple question of the non-equivalence of national languages—in this case, one that involves questions of "colonial differences".

We can now see, in any case, that Foucault's travels, after leaving France for Sweden in 1955, would become the start of long exercise in becoming foreign to the narrow preoccupations back in France—a long experiment in dis- and reorientation in his own thinking, carried on with others elsewhere, in an ever ongoing attempt to get away from his own assumptions and so become something of a "stranger to himself". At the same time, in these "other places", Foucault would often give brilliant public lectures on the changing debates in Paris, suggesting new ways their theoretical questions might be taken up in turn. Throughout the Japan Lectures, these two processes in his travels and his work would come together in many ways.

The publication of *Dits et écrits* in 1994 would serve to underscore precisely this dual process in his travels. François Ewald, Foucault's former assistant at the Collège de France, who teamed up with Daniel Defert on the project, would put it this way:

> The stay in Sweden was the first in a long series: Foucault, whose work, it is important to note, was not specially localized in France, throughout his life sought to multiply his trips (Poland, Germany, US, Canada, Brazil, Japan), each time finding a renewed occasion to decenter himself and to make himself a stranger to his own culture and, perhaps as well, from a more private point of view, to find the peace of anonymity.[7]

Japan would play a singular role in these larger processes. Ewald says that in the '50s and '60s, Foucault was uncertain that he wanted to pursue an academic career at all, instead toying with the idea of working as a sort of essayist and journalist abroad. It was with this in mind that he wanted to accept an offer, at the invitation of Maurice Pinguet, to become the Director of the Franco-Japanese Institute in Tokyo, giving up on the idea only because of his relationship with Daniel Defert, with whom he would instead go to Tunisia, and from where he would make later, in 1972, his first trip to Japan.[8] In Sidi Bou Said, he met a number of French journalists and publishers and then, in 1967, along with radical students, he took part in the demonstrations that gripped the country, which would completely alter the orientation—and diso-rientation—of his own work, giving it a new political cast.

Foucault long insisted that his own politicization occurred in Tunisia, and not in Paris, throughout his work retaining the sense that what took place in Paris in May '68 was part of a larger global move-ment, carried on in many different languages, political regimes, and economies at once—in Prague as well as Paris, in Mexico City as well as Berkeley or New York, in Beijing as well as Tokyo. It was thus itself a global or "transnational" movement, calling, Foucault thought, for an examination of the opposition to "power" that had brought the movements together. We thus discover themes running throughout the Japan Lectures regarding power and collective "will" or volition. It was precisely these sorts of questions that Foucault hoped to take up with two of his Japanese interlocutors, Maruyama and Yoshimoto, focused on the particular role Japan played in them. We now know that Maruyama had drawn up a detailed new history of "political intel-lectuals" in Japan with precisely this in mind;[9] and, in the Lectures, Foucault starts to ask what role Asian traditions, like Confucianism, for which there existed no exact "equivalent" in Europe, had played in this process. The very idea of the role of philosophy in opposing specific forms of power and of the State needed to be expanded, to include the long history of "Asian" traditions in them, and, therefore, in the new political movements.

The attempt to rethink the "function of the political intellectual" in Japan and more generally in Asia, given the new questions posed by the rise of new movements throughout the world, raised in turn a question about the corresponding kind of "transnational" space in which they might then proceed: through what kinds of critical journalism about what was going on, through what forms of academic translation and exchange? At the time, Foucault was very much engaged in just such problems.

In 1976, Foucault had already raised the question of the "function of the intellectual" in the political, and not merely sociological, sense of the term, drawing a contrast between two different figures: Emile Zola with his high-minded "universal" accusations during the Dreyfus Affair, and Robert Oppenheimer with his "specific" intervention from within the American military context, following the horrific spectacle of the bombing of Nagasaki and Hiroshima that he had worked to realize. But in the Japan Lectures, Foucault began to take up the question of the specificity of the political intellectual in an expanded field, outside France and America alone, focused on the singular case of postwar Japan. The question of such extra-European participation in the activity of critical thought was thus part of a larger attempt to rethink the very idea of the role of "the public" in critical thought, inside and outside Europe. What, in effect, would a transnational public space look like, and how could it be put in place?

In 1978, returning from Japan, in his lecture "What is Critique?" at the French Philosophical Society, Foucault began to raise such questions about the very idea of "the public" in the activity of critical thought and its destiny in Kant and his legacy. His analysis would form part of a whole series of lectures and interventions in different junctures and debates throughout his ongoing travels until the end.[10] How, asked Foucault, had Kant posed the question of "public reason", a journalistic debate carried on in a Berlin monthly over the question of enlightenment? How had it eventually led later to his remarks about the "enthusiasm" for Revolution in *The Conflict of the Faculties?* What did these two interventions have to do with the ways critical theory would "travel" after Kant across several national languages and traditions in Europe, leading up to what would shortly become a great French-German debate about "modernity", with America as a key bystander?

In Foucault's new reading and retelling of the travels of critical thought throughout the next two centuries in Europe, what mattered was the relation of the act of critique to the peculiar time in which it is made—the time of l'actuel. The term figures prominently throughout Foucault's Lectures in Japan where questions of "modernity" and therefore of "post-modernity" were raised in other ways than in the Franco-German-American debate. In effect it would become part of Foucault's own philosophical idiom or singular way of talking. In particular, it would give rise to a new project in global critical journalism, cutting across various national languages and related "public spheres".

Foucault began to use the term l'actuel in a specific way. In contrast to the old term "conjuncture" (supposing a totalized if "overdetermined" or "uneven" economic and political system and narrative), Foucault took the term from Nietzsche's Untimely Meditations (Unzeitgemasse Beträchtungen) in his essay on genealogy and history in 1971,[11] and then made it his own. L'actuel was, in effect, a prolongation of "the untimely" in Nietzsche. In his essay, Foucault had seen the untimely as a way of interrupting the model of history as memory supposed by an all-too-German "historicism", posing against it a kind of critical "counter-memory", which might be carried elsewhere, in other ways and in other languages. As such, it would lead to a new project that gradually came to fruition in Foucault: the invention of a kind of "philosophical journalism" of such moments of actualité. He started to imagine a new sort of global critical journalism based in such times of interruption and rethinking, linked in particular to the "counter-conducts" of dissident or disobedient practices of critical speech already to be found in Kant. "I am a journalist", he would start to interject or declare when asked about the nature of his own critical philosophy; and many of his interviews were in fact carried on with journalists, with whom he maintained relations. In his Preface to a book by the French journalist Jean Daniel, whom he had befriended in Tunisia, he was already suggesting the need for a new journalism of l'actuel.[12]

But in 1978, at the time of the Japan Lectures, the idea would assume a concrete new form, initiated by an Italian evening newspaper, which lead him to his own coverage of the Revolution (or in his terms, the "uprising") unfolding in Iran later that year. Assembling a group in Paris, and envisaging a whole series of such interventions, Foucault talked of a new kind of reportage of "Global" ideas shaking things up throughout the world outside the confines of national publics and related university and media spheres. Focused on "minorities or peoples", who until now have almost never been accustomed to speaking or to being heard, and to "the swarming of ideas on a global scale that stir things up everywhere", the project envisaged a new kind of transnational political journalism. As he put it:

> There are more ideas on earth than intellectuals often imagine. And those ideas are more active, more powerful and more stubborn than the politicians might think. We must be there to witness the birth of ideas and their explosive force, not in the books that announce them, but in the events through which they exhibit their force [...] intellectuals will work with journalists at the point of intersection of ideas and events.[13]

Even after his own fraught "reportage" on Iran,[14] the larger vision of a global critical space is to be found in his attempt to imagine a free or open space in Paris, as elsewhere, not of "human rights", but of the "rights of the governed.[15] It also is to be found in the furtherance of the new kinds of exchange in translation, publishing, and universities, which Foucault hoped to effectuate with Japanese intellectuals at the time. As he put it in the project "Des Travaux" that he had set up in Paris, it involved the "translations of foreign publications of which we have need in order to free up research in France", which would in turn form part of the kind of travail that could make "a meaningful difference in the field of knowledge, at the cost of a certain difficulty for the author and the reader, with the possible reward of a certain pleasure, in other words, of an access to another form of truth".[16]

In the Japan Lectures, Foucault raised such questions in a specific situation, and in a specific manner. What would such moments of critical actualité look like in particular in Japan and more generally in Asia, where the forces of colonialism and the anti-imperialist struggles against them had assumed a rather different form than in Europe? In what ways might they then figure in a philosophy of the future, yet to be invented, for which there exists no pre-given vocabulary or single national language, working instead through "encounters and reverberations" between Europe and non-Europe? How then might this new sort of collective will be actualized at this particular juncture in postwar, cold-war Japan? In what sense, in other words, was the question of "modernity" in Japan and for political intellectuals in Japan, not simply a European but also at the same time an Asian matter?

Such questions run throughout the Lectures and the ways we look back on what was at stake in them today. They form part of what Foucault sometimes called "the enigma of Japan"—that this great postwar nation, while as technologically advanced as any in Europe, nevertheless retained, especially in its sexual and religious practices, many non-European Asian attitudes and traditions, themselves mobilized in the Asian theater of the War and its traumatic aftermath in Japan. In effect, the defeat and the new American presence in postwar Japan were inseparable from the defeat of an earlier nationalist Japanese imperialism and colonialism, which had begun to take shape, Maruyama argued, in the Tokugawa Shogunate, but which, after 1945, had been recast along "cold-war" lines throughout the region. Hence the "enigma" of Japanese modernity and the need for new histories and forms of critical thinking, not only in Japan, but also in Europe.

In raising such questions Foucault rarely used the term "Asia", instead relying on the "vague, unpleasant to use, yet almost indispensable"[17] vocabulary of Occident and Orient. In his uses of that terminology, a key focus was on what, in English, we usually refer to as "West" and "East" Europe (or "West" and "East" Germany) with which Foucault had an ongoing intellectual engagement and renewed critical interest at the time. How then could one cross such cold-war borders in our ways of thinking, not simply in Europe but also at the same time in Asia, following, notably, the still fraught borders resulting from the "Korean War" with China in the '50s? Foucault would raise just such questions in a striking interview with the two Embassy officials responsible for his trip to Japan, conducted in Paris and published in Japanese in 1982, under the title "The First Step of the Colonization of the Occident".[18] While dissidence in Prague in '68 was still a Soviet matter, Foucault argued, with the emergence of Solidarity in Poland at the time, it had become a European one as well, part of a new sort of "imbrication of economies with military power", with implications for postwar Japan, and in particular, of course, for the singular fate of its military.

Today of course the old "binaries" of Orient and Occident, East and West, have long seemed unsustainable, giving rise to new critical histories, and new ways of studying and imagining Asia. How then should we translate them? In this volume, we have opted for using the terms "East" and "West" with caps to translate "Orient" and "Occident" in the text, suggesting that they are deliberate constructs, rather as with the current term "Black" with caps in American English. Today the terms "Asia" (and "Asian Studies") are now increasingly used for what, at the time when Foucault was writing, was, for better or worse, called "The Orient" (and "Oriental" or "Orientalist" studies). The "Far East" and the changing forms of sinology investigating it have long had a different history and imagined a rather different Orient than that of the "Near East" that Foucault had encountered in Tunisia; and of course now, the whole European geography of "Far" and "Near" no longer makes sense.

"Foucault in Asia" thus names in effect a complex and entangled problem which Foucault was grappling with at the time in his attempt to use the existing terminology of Occident and Orient in a *transnational* sense, transported to a world now increasingly confronted with a rise of new forms of Asian nationalism, already found at the time in what Singapore was calling "Asian values". Today we know as well that in 1978, when Foucault was lecturing in Japan, in China, following Deng Xiaoping's reforms, the very idea of "Asia"—and related "politics of imagining Asia"—would assume a singular new transnational role going back to the fraught history of China in the 20th century. In the 21st century, we are confronted in turn with a new assertion of "Asia" in Mainland China in a struggle with America and "the West", enlisting "the Rest" in the wake of the ignominy of two centuries of European colonialism and imperialism. Can we then now see "Asia" in the critical way Foucault at the time was trying to see "The Orient" not as the name of an imagined nation, but, on the contrary, as calling for the invention of new transnational forms of critical thinking, cutting across such imagined national borders, at the time caught up in cold-war divisions that Foucault sensed were already in crisis—as perhaps with "the new cold war" of today.[19]

Foucault had in fact articulated just such a critical transnational approach to talk of Occident and Orient at the time of an extended interview he gave in in Brazil, published on the eve of his trip to Japan, at almost the same moment as his interview with Shiguéhiko Hasumi, which opens this volume. Entitled "Power, A Magnificent Beast",[20] it not only sets out in some detail the sort of game Foucault would play using the terms Occident and Orient in his Japan Lectures, but also identifies a new problem and related critical reversal—that of the specious universality of modern Western ways of thinking, and, in response to it, the critical specificity of extra-European histories of encounter and exchange. The very idea of "Western philosophy" spreading from Greece to modern Europe in a great monolithic march had to be rethought, freeing the role of "non-Western" forms of thinking from all being "premodern" and giving them a new critical role. Far from dominating this history, talk of Orient and Occident had assumed many different forms in it, according to the ways European and non-European ways of thinking had come in contact with one another.

How then, in 19th-century Europe, did this peculiar talk assume a form that would then be spread throughout the world, assuming a de facto universality, leading to the question of new sorts of encounters and reverberations between Europe and non-Europe in a critical philosophy yet to be invented? It is the unwritten history of this spread that makes this "vague, unpleasant way of talking" almost indispensable—why there preexists no other; why we need to rethink the practice and idea of critical theory to deal with it.

In fact, the sort of "anti-colonialist" challenges to the supposed universality of Western thought are of recent origin, preceded by many earlier moments of interaction not yet dominated by Europe or European ideas in the same way. In the interview, setting aside "Asia, which is a yet another problem", Foucault draws attention to the situation of two great universalist religions in the Mediterranean, about which he asks:

> why is it that the Muslim world, the Muslim religion, that seemed to have, that indeed had, until the 12th and 13th centuries, a dynamism that was infinitely greater, stronger than Christianity, whose religious, military, social and cultural forms seemed much more supple, richer, more welcoming than in the Christian world of the High Middle ages, why is it that, after it a certain moment, everything was upended?[21]

How in the current situation, should we deal with our vague, unpleasant almost indispensable way of talking about and imaging East and West, Orient and Occident? By "Occident", Foucault declared what he meant was:

> that sort of small portion of the world, whose strange and violent destiny was ultimately to impose its ways of seeing, thinking, saying and doing on the entire world. [...] It's true that the world revolted against this Occident, that it has separated itself from it [...] it succeeded in making it lose its pre-eminent position, but that doesn't take away from the fact that the instruments that were used in the entire world to diminish the Occident and shake off its yoke, were created almost entirely by this very same Occident.[22]

In the Japan Lectures, Foucault would challenge this de facto universality, born of a violent colonial history in a number of different ways, found not simply in the critical debates about "modernity" in postwar Japan, but in terms of his own changing views. While much of his work had been focused on "modern Europe", in this period Foucault had started to abandon this focus, looking back earlier, in his study of modern sexuality in particular, to the singular role played by Christian practices. He would eventually abandon the six-volume study of sexuality in modern Europe that he had originally projected, drawing on new scholarship, and working from a new angle on the "problematization" of various conceptions ideas of sexual experience in ethical practices. To the publication of the new volumes of this expanded history, hastily brought together as he was dying, he would add a remarkable Introduction, explaining how he came to "modify" his original project, and in the process, reformulate his earlier ways of thinking. It is in this striking Introduction—more than in the two new volumes themselves—that we find the questions that Foucault was exploring in the Japan Lectures, where the question of modern sexuality was looked at from outside Europe. At the same time, throughout the Lectures, Foucault is trying to sort out a new problem in his work. Often in response to particular questions, we find him casting about for new ideas, trying out new hypotheses, in a public effort to *penser autrement* (think in other ways)—or, as he would put it, to *se déprendre de soi-même* (get away from himself) through the "game of truth", the only sort of critical "curiosity" worth pursuing. In particular, we find this restless activity in two areas: sexual politics and Marxism.

At the time, the Introduction to his new six-volume *History of Sexuality* had not yet been translated and the difficulties it had led him to in France were unknown in Japan. *The Order of Things* was the work Japanese readers were mostly familiar with. For the purposes of the Lectures, Watanabe provided advance excerpts from the Introduction, opening a discussion of how the questions Foucault was raising might look like from a Japanese point of view. "Modern sexuality" in Japan was not in fact entirely European. It had inherited from China an "erotic art" very different from the resulting "sexual science" in Europe, and had developed its own distinctive spaces of gay interaction.[23] Foucault's new history had been focused on what he called "the modern deployment (*dispositif*) of sexuality" which had taken hold in Europe in the 19th century, and was then being contested in new sexual movements in Paris, in ways Foucault had hoped to intervene, replacing talk of repression and liberation with a new "politics of truth". Not everyone was pleased; on the contrary, it marked something of a moment of "de-solidarization" in Foucault's relations with a number of different figures and groups, leading him to shift his focus and retell the story of how this "modern European sexuality" had arisen in the first place, and the forms it had assumed.

What then would the peculiar idea of "sexuality" modern Europe had invented for itself look like in the rather different context of modern Japan, where this European *dispositif* was not given, but transported?

How, more generally, might one then perceive the odd, normalizing, confessional sort of sexuality Europe had invented for itself in the 19th century in places other than Europe? In what sense does critical theory in sexual politics then become a "transnational" matter, assuming different forms in different places, rather than something just imported from France, or from the United States? What, in consequence, would it mean to include such other places, with their other histories and their "multiple temporalities" in the very idea and history of sexual (and feminist) movements, imagining new forms of alliance or intersection? Throughout the Japan Lectures as perhaps nowhere else, Foucault would explore such questions. Foucault had begun working on the singular role Christianity—and its "Pastorate"—would play in the constitution of a modern European sexuality. But what would this feature look like in places where Christianity had been introduced through missionary work, with its eventual relations with the larger colonialist spread of Western modernity and ways of thinking, and where other rather different sorts of "spiritual" and related sexual practices still prevail?

These problems intersect with another question that runs throughout the Lectures: the question of what to get rid of—and not get rid of—from Marx and from Marxism in the new kind of critical theory he was trying to formulate and experiment with in discussion with his Japanese interlocutors. If psychiatry and thus psychoanalysis would assume rather different forms in Japan than in Europe, the same is true of Communism and its relations with Marxism. In Japan as elsewhere, neither psychoanalysis nor Marxism, nor therefore the relations between the two, assumed the same forms as in Europe, in particular after the War, which so dramatically transformed their geographies, for example in Latin America. In the criticism of Freudo-Marxism in the Introduction to his *History of Sexuality*, Foucault was in effect challenging the link between the two in European sexual politics, extending it more subtly to the Parisian forms of "Lacano-Althusserism" and of "Lacan-Bataille" transgressive politics. How then should we think of Marx and Communist Parties in postwar Europe, and at the same time, in Japan or in Asia? Foucault would take up just such questions in what seemed to him a larger crisis in both countries, of the post and cold-war role played by Communist Parties.

In Foucault's multiple engagements with Marxist philosophy and critical history, the Japan Lectures play a singular if unrecognized role. Along with a related interview Foucault gave at the same time in Italy, now translated as "Remarks on Marx", in the Lectures we find one of the most explicit discussions of Marx and Marxism in his work, and certainly one that goes further in raising the question outside Europe.[24] In the history of the larger global or transnational ambitions of Marxism, Foucault thought a key role was played by the dream of World Revolution and the ways it had been directed against European imperialism. But given the outcome of the October Revolution, at the time very much in question in Asia as elsewhere, it was precisely that idea that needed to be rethought, and the story recast or retold. In relation to the perceived failure of the Revolution at the time, Foucault tried to substitute for the idea of Reform, a new contrast between uprisings (soulèvements) in different times and places and the grand Revolutionary Romance in which they had so long been enclosed, leading to "an impoverishment in political imagination". Starting with such unforeseen "events", could one find ways of reimagining political questions, opening up new ways of acting in common? Is it then, after all, as he would put it, not useless to rise up in revolt?

Such was the context in which Foucault in the Japan Lectures and in the related interview in Italy would review in some detail his own relations with Marx and with Communist Parties and States. Marx's great critique of political economy in the 19th century and the critical role "the proletariat" would play in response to it, would be the start of long, changing, ongoing history, in which Foucault at the time was drawn in particular historical writings, like the "18th Brumaire" and "Civil War in France", through which that analysis was combined with the political questions in the present. But the "event" Marx thus introduced in the midst of the 19th century would not stay the same. Capitalism itself, and the role of political economy in it, would assume new (and "globalizing") forms in the process, and so too the political question of how to respond to it. We need to see Marxist discourse and politics in the context of this long-changing, material history. It is thus not that Marx is dead, haunting us like a strange specter, calling for a new messianism, but is instead a thing of this world, where it would assume many changing forms, in which questions of State and Party would play a key and ongoing political role. No new reading of Marx, no retrospective discovery of the "true Marx", can ever change that history and the real role it would play in the lives of people; on the contrary, it is just that history that leads to new ways of reading Marx and Marxism. As Wang Hui has recently argued, after 1911, the destiny of Revolution in China, in particular, would play a singular role in this evolving global history and the ways, in which, far from being over, it is still with us today in the midst of the 21st century.[25] We need, in short, to think in terms of the "actualities" of Marx rather than a grand foreseeable Future, around which all critical thought, all political mobilization and imagination, would be focused. That is perhaps what makes Foucault's Marx a Marx for today.

The Japan Lectures capture a singular moment in Foucault's thought and his itinerary, carried on in many ways at once with a vital sense of play and freedom. Their republication and current retranslation are in turn part of the wealth of materials he left behind, which, retrospectively, has made his work seem more multiple, less contained in the earlier frameworks that had seemed to organize it, suggesting new uses and readings. In particular, in the Lectures we now find an unrealized project Foucault was trying at once to formulate, implement, and discuss with his Japanese interlocutors—an experiment in transnational critical thought and exchange. What should we make of it, what does it mean for the critical legacies or uses of his thought? Foucault's work was unfinished in a rather direct sense. It was cut off, rather suddenly, by an epidemic, of which the least one can say is that it was poorly understood at the time, leaving behind many unfinished works and projects. But Foucault's work can be said to be unfinished in a second sense, already to be found in his own thinking at the time. Critical philosophy, he came to see, is an activity that is intrinsically unfinished, predetermined by no final end or fixed beginning, instead constantly interrupted by new events and new questions, which, unforeseen, require it to be recast, reimagined, reoriented—exactly how, where, and by whom being not given in advance, instead forming part of the larger process, the larger experiment, at once subjective and collective. It is only in that way that critical thought lives on, taken up later, in new ways and new moments of collective "will" that arise in response to what is happening to us. It is then perhaps, in this second sense, that the transnational "philosophy of the future" Foucault evoked in 1978 in an off-hand response to a question posed by a curious Zen monk, has become a philosophy of today, a philosophy for us today.

NOTES

1 "Michel Foucault and Zen: A Stay in a Zen Temple" (see Lecture 8).
2 Michel Foucault, "Omnes et Singularum: Towards a Criticism of 'Political Reason", in The Tanner Lectures on Human Values, ed. Sterling M. McMurrin (Salt Lake City: University of Utah Press, 1981), p. 223–254.
3 Gilles Deleuze, "What is a dispositif?", in Michel Foucault, Philosopher (Routledge, 1992), p. 164 ff. In an earlier version in Foucault (Minnesota, 1986), p. 115, Deleuze associates the idea the political movements in various countries leading up to 1968 in Paris, which would "rehearse" these questions.
4 "An Interview with Steven Riggens", in Michel Foucault, The Essential Works of Michel Foucault, Vol 1, ed. Paul Rabinow (The New Press, 1977).
5 In The End of Pax Americana (Duke University Press, 2022), Naoki Sakai republishes the inaugural exchange with Jon Solomon in an updated history, focused on a new formation that emerged after the postwar moment when Foucault gave his Lectures—the rise of what he proposes to call "Northeast Asia" and the role of Japan's "reclusive withdrawal" (hikkomori) in it. A key event in this would be the defeat of Japanese imperialism, already debated at the time by Maruyama and Yoshimoto. For his part, Jon Solomon would update his views in "Foucault, 1978: The Biopolitics of Translation and the Decolonization of Knowledge" in Materiali Foucaultiani, Vol VI, number 11–12 (January–December 2017).
6 Sandro Mezzadra, "En voyage: Foucault et la critique postcoloniale", in Les Cahiers de L'Herne, Michel Foucault, 2011. My translation. This issue includes a number of discussions of Foucault in Asia, notably one by Hidekata Ishida, the Japanese editor of Dits et écrits.
7 François Ewald, "Repères biographiques', Magazine Littéraire, no. 325, October 1994, p. 21. My translation.
8 David Macey, The Lives of Michel Foucault (Random House, 1993), pp. 146–148. Daniel Defert, who played a key role in Foucault's politicization in Tunisia, and in the subsequent creation of the Group for Information on Prisons was involved in another aspect of Foucault's relations with Asia: the question of Maoism. Defert would in fact travel to Beijing, shortly after the notorious Tel Quel trip—from which Roland Barthes recoiled in horror—and he would later contribute to a special issue of Les Temps Modernes (no. 380, March 1978) devoted to China at a time of

increasing debate about Maoism. In his contribution, entitled "La Chine toujours édifiante et curieuse", he tried to situate the Simon Leys–Maria Macciochi debate of the day in the larger history of exchanges with Europe, going back the Jesuit missionaries at the end of the 17th century, where questions of travel, translation, and sources of knowledge were also at issue.

9 Maruyama's detailed history is part of the materials from Foucault's trip, which can now be consulted at IMEC. See the presentation of the interview with Shiguéhiko Hasumi in this volume.

10 Foucault would explicitly return to these questions in his last Courses, in association with a new analysis of the costs of "speaking freely" (parrhesia) in the "cosmo-political" (or transnational) practices of the Cynics.

11 Michel Foucault, "Nietzsche, Genealogy, History".

12 Michel Foucault, "Préface" to Jean Daniel's L'ère des ruptures (Grasset, 1979). Foucault had met Jean Daniel, the publisher of the French magazine Le Nouvel Observateur in Sidi Bou Saïd. In The Lives of Michel Foucault, op. cit,, David Macey describes the context of their encounter (pp 184–185).

13 "Les "reportages d'idées", Dits et écrits, Vol III, no. 250, pp 706–707. My translation.

14 Foucault in Iran: Islamic Revolution after the Enlightenment (Minnesota University Press, 2016), Berooz Ghamari-Tabizi offers a corrective to the responses to Foucault's intervention at the time. Himself a participant in the events in question, he uses Foucault's distinction between "uprising" and "Revolution" to reconstruct an early "protest" moment in the mass movement and the role of women and Iranian intellectuals in it.

15 "Confronting Governments: Human Rights", Libération, June 1984. Foucault associates the "rights of the governed" (as distinct from "human rights") with a new kind of "international citizenship".

16 Georges Canguilhem uses this description of the project "Des Travaux" to introduce the international symposium, Michel Foucault, philosophe, held in Paris in January 1988. In his presentation, Canguilhem associated the project with Foucault's Introduction to Uses of Pleasure, where he talks of a "game of truth" that would be foreign to dogmatic as well as to critical philosophies. He adds that the time had come to apply this spirit to Foucault's own work, his own philosophy.

17 "Le pouvoir, une bête magnifique", Dits et écrits, Vol III, no. 212, pp 368 ff. My translation.

18 "Rekishi henro kaiki" ("Un Premier pas de la colonisation de l'Occident"), Dits et écrits, Vol IV, no. 309, pp 261 ff. My translation.

19 Wang Hui, The Politics of Imagining Asia (Harvard University Press 2011).

20 "Le pouvoir, une bête magnifique", op. cit. My translation.

21 For the question of Asia, which Foucault sets aside, one could imagine looking first at the long history of the Silk Road in facilitating exchanges with Asia, then, in the postwar period, in the new initiatives crossing cold-war borders opened up in Bandung, Indonesia, and perhaps then, today, with the debates about the "neo-colonial" practices of the current Belt and Road policy.

22 "Le pouvoir, une bête magnifique", op. cit. My translation.

23 In 1978, together with Jean Le Bitoux, Foucault helped create a new publication called Gai Pied. In an interview in the inaugural issue, and in his subsequent interventions, Foucault takes up the issue of "space" in sexual practices, referring on several occasions to such spaces in Japan, thus continuing in an Asian context

the questions he had raised in the '60s about "other spaces". These interventions would later form part of a renewed interest in Foucault's views about gay sexuality, see David M. Halperin, "Jean Le Bitoux, and the Gay Science, lost and found", *Critical Inquiry*, vol. 37, no. 3 (Spring 2011), pp. 371–380.

24 Michel Foucault, *Remarks on Marx: Conversations with Duccio Trombardori*, Semiotext(e), 1991.

25 Wang Hui on the singularity of Revolution in China: "Twentieth Century in China as an Object of Thought: An Introduction, Part I The Birth of the Century: The Chinese Revolution and the Logics of Politics" in *Modern China*, 2020, vol. 46, pp. 3–46.

THE JAPAN LECTURES

1

POWER AND KNOWLEDGE

"Kenryoku to chi" ("Pouvoir et savoir"), interview with S. Hasumi recorded in Paris on October 13, 1977, in Umi, December 1977, pp. 240–256.

Dits et écrits III, no. 216

S. Hasumi: The public's interest in your work has increased considerably in Japan in these last few years, because following the highly anticipated translation of The Order of Things came Discipline and Punish, published two years ago, and then a part of La volonté de savoir that has recently been translated. Yet in the Japanese intellectual milieu there exist a number of Foucault myths that make an objective reading of your work impossible. These myths convey three mistaken images of you that are nonetheless generally accepted as true.

The first myth is that of a structuralist Foucault, killing off History and Man, as I told you in our previous interview. The second is that of a Foucault man of method, a myth that took hold in Japan after the translation of The Archeology of Knowledge. It is because of this book that you were received in some sense as the prodigal child of philosophy who,

DOI: 10.4324/9781003303763-3

after having wandered into the dubious field of literature had returned to a serious reflection on method. The third myth is that of a radical Foucault. You are considered radical because you talk about prisons and prisoners. One then expects that your *History of Sexuality* will be a subversive book as well. Do these myths also exist in France?

M. Foucault: They are widespread in France, and also in the United States. Two days ago, I received an article that was in fact very well done, by someone who took up my various books in their chronological order and who presented them, I would say with great objectivity, from *History of Madness* to *History of Sexuality*. The picture given of each book wasn't wrong, but I was absolutely stunned when at the end of this presentation the author wrote: "So you see, M. Foucault is a disciple of Lévi-Strauss, he's a structuralist, and his method is completely antihistorical or a-historical!" But to present *History of Madness*, to present *The Birth of the Clinic*, *History of Sexuality*, *Discipline and Punish* as ahistorical books is something I can't understand. And I will simply add that there has not been a single commentator, not one, who noticed that in *The Order of Things*, which is taken to be my structuralist book, the word "structure" isn't used even once. If it's mentioned in a quotation, it isn't said by me, not the word "structure" nor any of the concepts by which the structuralists define their method. It's therefore a very widespread prejudice. This misunderstanding is starting to dissipate in France, but to be honest I would have to say that there was a reason for it, because for a long time much of what I was doing wasn't entirely clear to me either. It's true that I was searching in a number of somewhat different directions.

One could, of course, reconstruct a sort of guiding principle. My first book was about the history of madness, which is to say the history of medical knowledge as well as the history of medical and psychiatric institutions. From there I went on to an analysis of medicine in general and also of medical institutions, dating from the beginning of modern medicine, and then to the study of empirical sciences like natural history, political economy, and grammar. All that is a sort of, I can't say a logic, but a progression by juxtaposition. But beneath this development that was free yet nonetheless plausible, there was something I didn't quite understand myself that was essentially this: what was it in fact that I was after?

For a long time I thought that what I was searching for was a kind of analysis of the fields of knowledge that come to exist in a society such as ours. What do we know about madness? What do we know about illness? What do we know about the world, about life? But I don't think that that was my real question. My real question, which is in fact now everyone's question, is that of power. I think we have to go back to the '60s, to what was going on at that time, let's say in 1955, because it was around then that I started my work. There were fundamentally two great historical legacies of the 20th century that we hadn't yet assimilated, and for which we lacked an analytic tool. Those two dark legacies were Fascism and Stalinism. The 19th century had encountered, as its major problem, the problem of poverty, of economic exploitation, of the formation of wealth, of capital, built upon the poverty of the very people who were producing this wealth. This enormous scandal had given rise to new reflections on the part of economists and of historians who had tried to solve it, to justify it as best they could, and, at the heart of all this, there was Marxism. I think that at least in Western Europe—and maybe also in Japan—that is to say in industrially developed countries, it wasn't so much the problem of poverty that was a stake, but the problem of an excess of power. There had been either capitalist regimes, as in the case of Fascism, or Socialist, or claiming to be Socialist, which was the case of Stalinism, in which the excess of power of the state apparatus, of the bureaucracy, but I would also say of individuals over one another, made for something that was absolutely revolting, as revolting as the poverty of the 19th century. The concentration camps we experienced in all those countries were, for the 20th century, what the notorious working-class cities, working-class slums, working-class mortality had been for the contemporaries of Marx. Yet there was nothing in the conceptual or theoretical tools that we possessed that allowed us to fully grasp this problem of power, since the 19th century, from which we had inherited those tools, had only understood these problems from an economic perspective. The

19th century had assured us that the day these economic problems would be solved, all the effects of excessive power would be solved as well. The 20th century discovered the opposite: no matter how well we solve all the economic problems, the excesses of power still remain. Around 1955, the problem of power had started to fully reveal itself. I would say that until then, until 1955, one could have thought—and that's exactly what the Marxists told us—that if Fascism with its excess of power could have occurred, and even, one could say, if the excesses of Stalinism could have occurred, it was because of the economic difficulties capitalism had gone through in 1929, and that the Soviet Union had gone through during the difficult period of the years between 1920 and 1940. But in 1956, something happened that I think was crucial and decisive: with Fascism having disappeared as an institutional form in Europe, with Stalin dead, and Stalinism wiped out, or supposedly wiped out, by Khrushchev in 1956, the Hungarians revolt in Budapest, the Russians step in, and Soviet power, which in fact was no longer pressured by economic necessity, reacted as we have seen. At the same time, in France, we had the Algerian War, and that was very important, because there again, we saw that despite all the economic problems, French capitalism showed that it could easily do without Algeria, without the colonization of Algeria—what we were dealing with were mechanisms of power that sort of got carried away on their own, beyond fundamental economic pressures. Hence the necessity to think about this problem of power, but the lack of conceptual tools to do so. I think that basically, and a bit unconsciously, people of my generation, and I'm only one of them, ended up trying to figure out this phenomenon of power. At this point I would retrospectively reconstruct my work essentially in terms of this problem.

What was *History of Madness* about? An attempt to identify not so much the kind of knowledge that we came to conceive as mental illness as the kind of power that reason has endlessly sought to exercise over madness from the 17th century until now. In the thing I did on *The Birth of the Clinic* it was this same problem once again. In what way did the phenomenon of illness constitute for society, for the State, for the developing institutions of capitalism, a sort of challenge that had to be met through the means of the institutionalization of medicine, of hospitals? What status was given to the sick? That's what I also wanted to do for prisons. Hence a whole series of analyses of power. I would say that *The Order of Things*, beneath its literary, purely speculative appearance, if you will, is also a bit that, a search for the mechanisms of power within scientific discourses themselves: what rule must be followed at a given time in order to produce a discourse on life, on natural history, on political economy? What must be obeyed, to what constraints is one subjected, how, from one discourse to another, from one model to another, are effects of power produced? So it's that whole connection between knowledge and power, with mechanisms of power being the central focus, that is, essentially, what I wanted to do. Which is to say it has nothing to do with structuralism and it is very clearly a history—whether I succeeded or not, it's not up to me to judge—a history of mechanisms of power and how they were set in motion.

It is certain that I don't have, any more than other people of my generation, a ready-made tool with which to construct all this. I try to start from precise empirical studies on a specific topic, in a specific field. I don't have a general and all-encompassing conception of power. I imagine someone will come after me and do that. I myself don't do it.

S. Hasumi: So, the fundamental problem for you, starting with your first book, *History of Madness*, is always the problem of power.

M. Foucault: That's right.

S. Hasumi: Yet you have never, or only rarely, spoken of what is called the class struggle or infrastructure, as a way of tackling this problem. So from the start it was clear to you that an analysis inspired by Marx was no longer useful for this sort of phenomenon.

M. Foucault: Let's take the case of *History of Madness*, the field I was engaged in at that time. Two things were certain: on one hand, mad people don't constitute one class and reasonable people another. You can't superimpose the series of confrontations that can transpire on one side or another of the line that separates reason from unreason. That's obvious, no need for commentary. Yet it needs to be said. On the other hand, it is certainly the case that the institutionalization of certain types of practices such as internment, the organization of psychiatric hospitals, the difference that exists for example between internment in a hospital and the care a patient can receive in a clinic—all those differences are undoubtedly linked to the existence of class in the Marxist sense. But the way this confrontation between the classes is manifested in the areas I study is extremely complicated. It is only through a whole lot of very different, entangled, and unclear paths that you can uncover the real connection between class relations and the workings of an institution such as a regular hospital or a psychiatric one.

More simply, or more clearly put: at the heart of the mechanisms of confinement that arose throughout Europe during the 16th, but mainly the 17th century, we find the problem of joblessness, of people who can't find work, who emigrate from one country to another, who circulate throughout the whole social sphere. Those people who had been liberated by the religious wars, then by the end of the Thirty Years' War, the impoverished peasants, all these make for a population adrift, a troubling one, the reaction to which was an attempt at a generalized confinement, in which mad people got caught as well. It's all very complicated, but I don't think it's very useful, that it's very productive to say of psychiatry that it's a psychiatry of class, of medicine that it's a medicine of class, that doctors and psychiatrists represent class interests. You get nowhere by doing that, but you nonetheless have to reinsert the complexity of these phenomena within historical processes, that are economic, etc. ...

S. Hasumi: About *History of Madness*, I remember that in the beginning of the '60s, Japanese scholars of French literature spoke of your book in the same way they did of *The Idea of Happiness* that was written in the 17th century by Robert Mauzi, as a sort of monothematic study of madness. We didn't foresee the impact the book would have ten years later. In Japan, we hadn't exactly understood its importance at the time, despite having read the chapter on the great confinement. We hadn't understood that your thinking was in fact always pointing in the same direction, but without having established a fixed method, which is so essential in your work and has led to some misunderstanding. For example, after the publication of *The Archaeology of Knowledge*, a lot was said about the Foucault method, but in fact you had never articulated one ...

M. Foucault: No, *The Archaeology of Knowledge* is not a book of methodology. I don't have a method that I then apply in the same way to different fields. On the contrary, I would say that I try to isolate a singular field of objects by using tools that I find or fabricate at the very same time as I'm doing my research, but without privileging the problem of method at all. In this sense as well, I am not at all a structuralist, because the structuralists of the '50s and '60s had as their main goal to define a method that was, if not universally valid, at least generally valid for a whole series of different objects: language, literary discourse, myths, iconography, architecture ... That isn't my preoccupation at all: what I try to do is to make visible the sort of layer, I was going to say interface, as would the modern technicians, the interface of knowledge and power, of truth and power. That's it, that's what I want to do.

There are truth-effects that a society, such as Western society, and now we can say society everywhere, produces at every moment. We produce truth. These productions of truths cannot be dissociated from power and mechanisms of power, both because these mechanisms of power make possible, in fact induce these productions of truths, and these productions of truths themselves have effects of power that bind us, tie us to one another. It's those truth–power, knowledge–power relations that interest me. But that layer of objects, or rather that zone of relations, is something difficult to apprehend, and, as there exists no general theory for apprehending them, I am, if you will, a blind empiricist, which is to say I'm in the worst situation possible. I have no general theory, and I don't have a reliable tool either. I feel my way, I construct, as best I can, instruments that are intended to make objects appear. The objects are a bit determined by the instruments—be they good or bad—that I create. They are wrong if my instruments are wrong ... I try to correct my instruments through the objects I think I discover, and then, the corrected instruments reveal that the object I had identified wasn't exactly what I thought it was. And that's how I flounder, or stumble, from one book to the next.

S. Hasumi: You have just used an expression that is very important in terms of defining your attitude towards your research: "blind empiricist". I in fact wrote an article about *The Archaeology of Knowledge* in which I say: "The most beautiful moment in the writings of Foucault is when he finds himself in a place of not-knowing and admits his helplessness when confronted with the complex relations between ideas and events". This place of not-knowing is not a deficiency that discourages you, but rather an almost existential necessity that compels you to think and that incites you to engage in a creative relationship with language. It's your very specific relationship with thought and language that causes a whole lot of misunderstandings. Normally, a method is established in advance, which then allows for the analysis of something unknown. You don't accept this relationship between known and unknown.

M. Foucault: That's it. Which is to say that generally, either you have a definite method for an object that isn't known, or the object preexists, you know it's there, but you think it hasn't been analyzed properly and you devise a method for analyzing this preexisting object that is already known. Those are the only two sensible ways of going about things. But I behave in a way that is absolutely unreasonable and pretentious, disguising it as humility, but it is in fact pretention, presumption, insane presumption, almost in the Hegelian sense, to want to talk about an unknown object with an undefined method. So I spread ashes on my head, that's the way I am.

S. Hasumi: So, in your book on sexuality …

M. Foucault: I'd like to add one thing. After what I just said, people might ask: "Why do you say anything at all, do you have a guiding principle or not?" Let me get back to what I was saying earlier about Stalinism. Currently there exist in our societies—and it's in this way that politics comes in—a certain number of questions, problems, wounds, worries, anxieties, that are the real motor for the choices I make and the objects I try to analyze and the way I try to analyze them. That's what we are: the conflicts, tensions, anxieties that run through our lives, which is ultimately the ground—I can't call it solid—because it is by definition a minefield, it is dangerous, the ground on which I travel.

S. Hasumi: So that's why you talk about power when you write *History of Sexuality*. But there again, I think there may be a misunderstanding, because the word "power" has always been associated, as it still is now, with the notion of the sovereignty of the State, whereas you try to define the word "power" in your book as being neither an institution, nor a structure, nor a state power, but a strategic place where all of the power–knowledge relations converge. I have the sense that you're talking about something other than power, that you're talking about what you call truth, not the truth that contemporary society produces everywhere, but the truth that you want to get at through the fiction of your work. I may be wrong, but doesn't your definition apply better to what you call truth?

M. Foucault: No, you're not wrong. I think I can say the same thing slightly differently by saying that in France, power is also generally understood as the effects of domination that are linked to the existence of a State and to the workings of the state apparatus. Power: what immediately comes to mind is the army, the police, the judicial system. As for sexuality: in the past, adultery and incest were condemned, now it's homosexuality and rapists. But if you have that conception of power, I think you locate it only within the state apparatus, even though power relations exist, and are to be found—something we in fact know but we don't always draw the consequences—in many other places as well. Power relations exist between a man and a woman, between one who knows and one who doesn't, between parents and children, within the family. In society there are thousands and thousands of power relations, and, consequently, relations of force that lead to small confrontations, micro-struggles so to speak. If it's true that these small power relations are very often enforced, induced from above by the large powers of the State or by large class domination, it also has to be said that conversely, the domination by a class or a state apparatus can only function properly if there exist, underlying it, all those small power relations. What would state power be, the power that imposes military service for example, if you didn't have, surrounding each individual, a whole cluster of power relations that bind them to their parents, their employers, their masters—to the one who knows, to the one who has stuffed their mind with some idea or other?

The state apparatus, inasmuch as it is something general, abstract, even violent, couldn't maintain its grip on us, continually and surreptitiously, if it weren't rooted in, if it didn't use as a sort of grand strategy all the small, localized and individual tactics that surround each one of us. That's it, it's a bit of this fundamental nature of power relations that I would like to bring to light. That's how I would answer what you were saying about the State. I would also like to show that these power relations use methods and techniques that are very, very different from one another, according to the time and the zone in which they occur. For instance, the police has its methods—as we well know—but there is also a whole method, a whole series of procedures through which the power of the father is exerted over his children, through which, within a family, power relations are formed, of parents over their children, but also children over their parents, of men over women, but also women over men, and over children. In each case with its specific methods, its specific technology. But it's also important to say that we can't think of these power relations as a sort of brutal domination in the form of "You have to do that or I'll kill you". That would only occur in extreme instances of power. In fact, relations of power are relations of force, confrontations, which can therefore always be reversed. There are no power relations that are entirely victorious and whose domination is inescapable. People often say—and critics have reproached me for this—that by seeing power everywhere, I eliminate any possibility of resistance. But it's the opposite!

What I mean is that power relations necessarily trigger, call for at every moment, the possibility of resistance, and it's because there's a possibility of resistance, and real resistance, that the dominant force tries to hold on to its power with ever more force, ever more ruse, as the resistance becomes stronger. It's therefore more the constant and multifaceted struggle that I try to expose than the grim and stable domination of a uniformizing apparatus. There are struggles everywhere.

There is, at every moment, the revolt of the child picking its nose at the table to annoy its parents—that's a rebellion one could say—and at every moment we go from rebellion to domination, from domination to rebellion, and it's this constant agitation that I would like to show. I don't know if I've exactly answered your question. There was the question of truth. By truth, I can certainly say that I don't mean a kind of generalized norm, a series of propositions. What I mean is the set of procedures that allow every person at every moment to produce statements that will be taken as true. There is absolutely no supreme authority. There are zones in which these truth-effects are perfectly coded, in which the procedures through which one comes to state these truths are known, settled in advance. That is the case, broadly speaking, in the scientific realm. In mathematics, it's absolute. In the case of sciences that are, let's say empirical, it's already a lot less clear. And then, outside of the sciences, you also have truth-effects that are linked to information networks: when someone, such as a speaker on the radio or on television, tells you something, either you believe it or you don't, but it starts to work in the minds of thousands of people as truth, only because it's said in that way, with that tone, by that person, at that time.

I'm by no means the first to have raised the question of power I was talking to you about earlier. Many very interesting people, and well before 1956, tried to study from a Marxist perspective what they called the bureaucratic phenomenon, which is to say the bureaucratization of the Party. That had been done in the early thirties in Trotskyite circles or in ones that derived from Trotskyism. They did important work. But the way I pose the problem is certainly different, because I don't look for the aberration that occurred in the state apparatuses that led to an increase of power. On the contrary, I try to see how, in daily life, in relationships between the sexes, within families, between the mentally ill and those considered sane, between the sick and their doctors—how in all that there are inflations of power. In other words, the inflation of power in a society such as ours doesn't have a single origin like the State and the bureaucracy of the State. As soon as there is this continual inflation, this rampant inflation, as economists would say, that is created at every moment, with almost every step we take, we can wonder: "But why, in that instance, am I exercising power? Not only by what right, but what for?" Take, for example, what happened to the mentally ill. For centuries people lived with the idea that if we didn't lock them up, it would be, first, dangerous for society, and second, dangerous for them as well. It was thought that we had to lock them up in order to protect them from themselves, and to prevent the social order from being compromised. But we are witnessing today a sort of generalized opening up of psychiatric hospitals—it's become quite systematic, I don't know about Japan, but certainly in Europe—and we are seeing that it doesn't increase the level of danger for rational people at all. Of course, the case of people who were released from psychiatric hospitals and who killed someone will be brought up, but if you look at the statistics, if you look at how things were before, there weren't more, I would even say there were fewer cases, than at the time when there was an attempt to lock up everyone, and when, even discounting evasions, there were still a whole lot of people who had never been locked up.

S. Hasumi: Going back to the idea of history, I'd like to know whether you have Gaston Bachelard in mind when you use the terms epistemological "break" or "rupture"?

M. Foucault: In a way, yes. Because there again, I started from an empirical observation. I don't think I used the word rupture in *History of Madness*. I used it for sure, or concepts similar to it, in *The Birth of the Clinic* and *The Order of Things*, because in those areas, which are scientific ones, and only in those, we can see, now as in the past—at least between the16th and the 19th century—a whole lot of sudden changes that belong to the order of observable facts. I challenge anyone who reads medical books, from the period that goes from 1750 to 1820 for example, not to see at a given moment and over a stretch of time—an extraordinarily short time frame of 15 or 20 years—a change, not only in theories, in concepts, in words, in vocabulary, but in the objects that are talked about—in the relation to things—a change that is radical and is the proof of an epistemological finding, such that when you read a medical book written by a good doctor from the years 1820 to1830, with your current medical knowledge, you know perfectly well what he's telling you. You might think: "Oh! he's mistaken about the causes. Oh! there he missed something. Oh! later microbiology would contribute this or that". But you know what he's talking about. When you read a book of medicine, even by a renowned doctor, from the years prior to 1750, 50 percent of the time you're made to wonder: "What sickness is he even talking about? What on earth is that? What does it correspond to?" When you read very good descriptions of epidemics, even very detailed ones, dating from the beginning of the 18th century, you're forced to think: "Well, it must have been some disease or other, but you can't be sure", which is proof that the perspective, the relation to things have changed. Once again, this takes the form of a break.

When you read *Natural History* of Buffon you understand very well what he is saying. Yet his way of dealing with things will be completely upended starting, roughly speaking, with Cuvier, which is to say 40 years later, when, in his *Comparative Anatomy*, Cuvier will be able to decipher structures, find analogies, classifications, organizations of a very different kind. There again, the break is immediately apparent. When I talk about a break, it's not at all that I'm making it a principle of explication; on the contrary, I try to identify the problem and then to say: let's assess all these differences, let's not erase these breaks by saying: "There has been continuity". On the contrary, let's assess all the differences, let's add them up, let's not minimize the existing differences and let's try to find out what happened, what has been transformed, what has been reduced, what has been displaced, what is the set of transformations that allow for the passage from one state of scientific discourse to another. All this applies to scientific discourses and takes place only in them. In other fields you don't have these abrupt mutations at all. For example, for *History of Sexuality*, I'm now looking at all the texts of the Pastorals and the Christian directives of conscience and I can assure you that since Saint Benedict, since Saint Jerome, since the Greek Fathers and especially since the Syrian and Egyptian monks, and up until the 17th century, there is extraordinary continuity, with, of course, some accelerations, some slowdowns, some moments of stabilization—there's a whole lot of activity there—but certainly no rupture. For me, the idea of rupture isn't at all a basic concept, it's an observable fact. And I've noticed that people who were knowledgeable about scientific literature weren't surprised at all when I talked about rupture. A historian of medicine doesn't deny this break.

S. Hasumi: When you talk about breaks, Marxist historians are shocked because you don't talk about the French Revolution ...

M. Foucault: They're funny ... It's absolutely true that I don't talk about it with respect to comparative anatomy; you can of course find some effects of the Revolution on the career of some professor or other in the museum, stuff like that, but that isn't the real problem. On the other hand, I do talk about the French Revolution, I was in fact obliged to do so, it would have been unseemly for me not to with respect to psychiatric institutions, since the structure of confinement, the institution of confinement, were completely transformed during the French Revolution. Marxist historians always forget to say that I've talked about the French Revolution with respect to that. They also forget to say that I talked about it with respect to medicine, because in medicine, God knows it was important: the dismantling of the corporative structures of the medical profession at the very time of the Revolution, all the projects for a kind of global, hygenicizing medicine, a medicine of health rather than of illness during the years 1790 to 1793, the importance of the Revolutionary and Napoleonic wars for the formation of a new medical corps—I've talked about all of that. Unfortunately, Marxists don't talk about the fact that I talked about it. But when, with respect to comparative anatomy, I don't talk about the French Revolution—and I think that's an incredible violation of someone's rights—they say: "You see! He never talks about the French Revolution".

S. Hasumi: In *History of Sexuality*, you do a very in-depth analysis of the role of confession in the West. Do you think that in a world where this science of sexuality doesn't exist, confession still plays a role?

M. Foucault: One would have to see. In Buddhism, there are confession practices for the monks that are very strictly defined. Buddhism therefore has structures of confession. It clearly doesn't have them on as large a scale as in Western Christianity, where everyone was subjected to the practice of avowal, where everyone was supposed to admit their sins and where millions of people, hundreds of millions of people were in fact obliged to admit their sins. On the formal level, when you look at the rules of Buddhist monasticism and the rules of Christian confession, you can find many analogies, but in reality, it didn't work in the same way at all.

S. Hasumi: Confession always takes the form of a narrative surrounding the truth of a crime or a sin. It could therefore have formal connections with other types of narratives: for example, adventures, tales of conquests, etc. Would you say that in modern society there is a narrative form that is specific to confession?

M. Foucault: Christianity has, if not invented, at least implemented a practice of avowal that is absolutely singular in the history of civilizations, a constraint that lasted for centuries. Starting with the Reformation, the discourse of confession sort of exploded instead of remaining confined within the ritual of penitence. It became a behavior that could have let's call it a purely psychological function, of a better knowledge of self, a better mastery of self, a reassessment of one's tendencies and the possibility of managing one's life—practices of self-examination that Protestantism greatly encouraged even beyond penitence and confession, and confession to the Pastor. One can also see, at that time, the growth of a literature written in the first person, in which people keep a diary in which they talk about their day, say what they've done—a practice that mainly developed in Protestant countries, even if there are some instances of it in Catholic ones. Then came that literature in which confession played such an important role—in France, The Princess of Clèves—a literature in which one's own adventures are narrated in a barely disguised, slightly fictional form. This extraordinary dissemination of the mechanism of confession is now coming to those shows in France—I imagine also in Japan—those radio shows soon followed by television, in which people come and say: "Yeah, well, you know, I don't get along with my wife, I can't make love to her anymore, I can't get an erection, I'm really embarrassed, what should I do …" The history of confession doesn't stop there,

there will be other twists and turns … This phenomenon is very significant and very specific, in its origins, to Western Christianity. In Japan, you now have this sort of phenomenon as well, but it came from the West. In traditional Japanese culture there wasn't this need for confession, this demand for confession that has been so strongly embedded by Christianity in the Western soul. That needs to be studied further.

S. Hasumi: In Japan, around the 1900s, there was an attempt to modernize the novel as a genre, whose supporters called for a literature of confession.

M. Foucault: Oh! Really?

S. Hasumi: This romantic literature of confession in the style of Jean-Jacques Rousseau even became a tradition in contemporary Japanese novels, oddly referred to as "naturalism"! There is now a whole literature of spontaneous confession. Strangely, it affected people who had never learned to read or write. For example, a prisoner on death row wrote novels of that sort in jail, as did Fieschi, who asked that everything he wrote be published without changing the spelling. Hence prison, writing, desire for confession …

M. Foucault: This is certainly an instance of what can be called a rupture. The stories of former delinquents, of prisoners, of people who were sentenced to death were practically non-existent before the beginning of the 19th century—we have seen very few examples of it. And then, starting in 1820, there are thousands of testimonies of prisoners who wrote, of people exhorting prisoners telling them: "Go ahead and write your recollections, give us your memoirs, give us your testimonies". Journalists would throw themselves at the feet of criminals in the hope they'd be willing to offer up their pronouncements. It's a very important and strange phenomenon that happened very quickly, but that's also linked to the old tradition according to which criminals had to be punished essentially on the basis of their confession. A criminal had to be made to confess. Even when there was evidence against him, you still had to get him to confess as a kind of authentication of the crime by the criminal himself. Moreover, at the beginning of the 19th century, the idea that the punishment of a crime had to lead to the correction, not the improvement, of the criminal, the transformation of his soul, entailed that this man be known and reveal himself. From the moment the punishment is no longer the response to a crime, but a transformative operation of a criminal, the discourse of the criminal, his confession, the revelation of who he is, what he thinks, what he desires becomes indispensable. It's a kind of calling mechanism if you will.

S. Hasumi: I'm thinking of a writer like Céline for example. Everything he has written since his return to France is a somewhat fake confession in which he recounts everything that's happened to him, everything he's done. Gaston Gallimard perfectly understood the public's appetite for avowals, for confession …

M. Foucault: For sure. In the West, sin is one of the fundamental experiences that triggers speech—more than exploits. But let's take the Greek heroes of The Iliad and The Odyssey. Neither Achilles nor Agamemnon nor Ulysses ever talks from the place of sin. Sometimes wrongdoing plays a part, but it isn't the triggering mechanism. One could say that today, on the contrary, it's on the basis of sin that the mechanism of incitement to discourse, and to literature as well, is triggered.

S. Hasumi: I notice that you have just used the word "literature". In the past you talked about it quite spontaneously and a lot.

M. Foucault: Oh, a lot, a lot … a little bit!

S. Hasumi: But still …

M. Foucault: The reason is very simple. At that time, I didn't really know what I was talking about. I was searching for the law or principle of my discourse, which I now understand better.

S. Hasumi: But precisely, couldn't one say that what you are doing now is closer to literature, and for that reason you no longer feel the need to talk about it? Because far from being discourses about truth, the purpose of your writings is to push the limits of thought and make visible what could be called the very body of language.

M. Foucault: I would like to be able to answer that it's true that truth isn't what concerns me. I talk about truth, I try to see how around discourses that are considered true, specific effects of power coalesce, but my real problem, in the end, is to create instruments of analysis, of political action and political intervention on the reality that we now live in, as well as on ourselves.

To take a very simple example: you were saying earlier that *History of Madness* was read as a monograph on a theme. Well, yes, that's all it was, and what happened? Very strangely, and not of my own doing, the fact of doing the history of the psychiatric institution, showing that the power mechanisms in which it was caught literally wounded the conscience of psychiatrists as to their practice, and alerted people to what was going on in psychiatric hospitals, so much so that this book, which is nothing more than a history of psychiatric institutions, true or false, useful or not, is considered a book of antipsychiatry, and I'm still attacked now, which is to say 16 years after its publication, as being one of those awful provocateurs who, unaware of the dangers and the risks to which they exposed themselves and others, were apologists for madness and antipsychiatry.

Translated by Anne Boyman

2

SEXUALITY AND POLITICS

"Sei to seiji wo kataru" ("Sexualité et politique"); interview with C. Nemoto and M. Watanabe, April 27, 1978, in Asahi Jānaru, v. 20 no. 19, May 12, 1978, pp. 15–20.

Dits et écrits III, no.230.

M. Watanabe: Mr. Foucault, today, April 27, you gave a very interesting lecture on "The Philosopher and Power in the Western World" in the Asahi lecture hall. In the coming editions of this review, we are going to publish a summary of your analysis of the role that Europe played in the technologies of power of the Catholic Church—what you call the "morphological power of the priest"—in the formation of both the individual and the dynamics of power whose object was the individual. As you are leaving for Paris tomorrow, this interview will be the last of your time in Japan and I'd like us to discuss sexuality and politics.

Now, one could say that sexuality and politics, or else sexuality and power, is the main theme of History of Sexuality that you are writing at the moment. The first volume, The Will to Knowledge, was already published

DOI: 10.4324/9781003303763-4

last year. I translated a part of it to be included in Chuō Koron's *Umi* and the translation of the entire work is in progress. I'd like to ask you a few questions regarding some of the proposals and hypotheses you presented in it.

A subject like sexuality and power immediately evokes the problems of censorship and then of sexual freedom, which are closely related to one another.

One of the most important ideas in *The Will to Knowledge* is that by talking so much about sexual liberation and the injustice of censorship, we miss the essence of the current phenomena surrounding sexuality. Notably, the repressive hypothesis distracts from the abnormal proliferation of discourse about sex. It is this very phenomenon, in fact, that is essential for analyzing the relationship between sexuality and power. All this is not to say that we underestimate the injustice of censorship, but it must be put into context as part of a larger apparatus of power.

Despite the lifting of bans on pornography by the government of President Giscard d'Estaing, I suppose that in France you have many systems of censorship and prohibition. In Japan, this works in a significantly more absurd way, to the extent that it's only natural that the prospect of sexual liberation be a goal for those who oppose power.

The standard of censorship is totally arbitrary, and it is obvious to us that it is a strategy of power. For example, you may have heard that censorship for images is excessive compared to speech; when it comes to images, the censorship is only aimed at pubic hair and sexual organs; whereas for discourse, exhibitionist texts intended for weekly publications are tolerated, while literary works are censored. Like your other works, *The Will to Knowledge* has clarified things that we have not precisely examined or accurately identified, even though we thought about them and could witness them in everyday life.

Furthermore, you put these things back in the context of their larger systems.

In Japan, on the one hand, there is the stupid censorship that prohibits importing even fashion magazines if pubic hair is not erased. On the other, we are inundated with talk about sex. I would like to come back to this later.

C. Nemoto: To begin, let's discuss In the Realm of the Senses (1975), a film by Nagisa Ōshima which was successful in France and made a name for itself because it was censored in Japan. Have you seen this film?

M. Foucault: Yes of course. I saw it twice.

C. Nemoto: Do you know what happened when the film was imported to Japan?

W. Watanabe: We saw the film divided in two in the middle of the screen as the forbidden parts had been cut out.

M. Foucault: I'm not very strong in anatomy and I can't quite imagine what it must have looked like, but that's outrageous.

M. Watanabe: And what was your impression of the film?

M. Foucault: I can't speak personally about the problem of prohibited and tolerated images in Japan nor the fact that in Japan what was shown in this film was considered particularly scandalous, as there's a completely different system of censorship in France. In any case, the system of censorship exists ... But I don't think that the images shown in the film are images that have never been shown before. This does not mean at all that it's an inconsequential film. When I speak of "images that have never been seen", I don't necessarily mean sexual images or images of sexual organs. In recent films, you can see the human body—the head, or the arm, or the skin—shown from a completely new angle and therefore from new points of view. In this film, we didn't see images that have never been shown.

And yet, I was very impressed by the form of the relationship between man and woman, more precisely by the relationship of these two people in relation to the man's genitals; this object is the link between the two of them, for the man as well as for the woman, and it seems to belong to both of them in a different way. The amputation that happens at the end of the film makes absolute sense and it is something that will never happen in French films or in French culture.

For the French, men's genitals are literally the symbol of manhood, and men equate themselves with their sexual organ and maintain a deeply intimate relationship with it. This is an indisputable fact and therefore women benefit from the male sex only if men grant them the right to do so; either they lend it to them or they impose it on them, from which follows the idea that male jouissance comes first and is essential.

In this film however, the male genital is an object that exists between the two characters and each has, in their own way, a right to this object. It is an instrument of pleasure for both of them, and since they derive pleasure from it—each in their own way—the one who derives more pleasure from it ends up possessing more rights to it. This is precisely why, in the end, the woman possesses this organ exclusively, it belongs only to her, and the man allows himself to be dispossessed of it. This is not castration in the habitual sense because the man was not up to the level of pleasure that his genitals gave to the woman and I think it's more accurate to say that he was detached from his organ, that his organ was detached from him.

W. Watanabe: Your interpretation is very interesting. If this event surpassed the category of sensationalized news to actually touch the imagination of the Japanese public at the time, and continues to today, it is perhaps because there is a mythic and collective illusion about the male sex that the Japanese have kept alive since ancient times. In any case, I think it's different from simple castration.

Regarding the repressive hypothesis and the multiplication of sexual discourses, as you explained in the seminar on "Sex and Power" at the University of Tokyo, the starting point of the history of sexuality was a comparison between the increase in hysterics in the end of the 18th century and new medical approaches to sexuality which developed in the19th. This means that on one hand, hysteria, which is an omission of sex, increases, while on the other, the effort to describe all manifestations of sex with a discourse on sexuality escalates.

In this you find the attitude of the Western world toward sex dating back to the Middle Ages, since which time it has been understood as a field of knowledge that you call the *scientia sexualis*. Conversely, you believe that in ancient Greece, in the Roman Empire, and in Asia, sex was seen from another angle and was practiced as an *ars erotica* to reinforce and increase the pleasures of sexual acts.

You say yourself that this division is only one example. Since the Meiji era, Confucian asceticism and a certain Protestant asceticism have produced taboos that were previously unknown to the Japanese. We do not live at all according to the principle of pornographic engravings and there are things that are considered perverted in our society without religious or legal prohibition, homosexuality for example. In such a society, sexual prohibition and incitement cannot be explained in a simple way, because it is related to the stratified structure of recorded history. Sex in Japan, before modernization and thus before Europeanization, seemed to fall into the realm of an *ars erotica*, but now it has entered into a curious relationship with the *scientia sexualis* of Europe. For example, if you look at women's magazines, they are replete with a discourse reflecting the principle of European-style sexual liberation: the more you know about sex the greater the guarantee of sexual fulfillment. Beginning with special features such as "Everything you don't know about the male body" and ending with "What you don't know about homosexuality", the insertion of the subject of sex within discourse is practiced whenever possible. Moreover, this category of discourse is limited to magazines aimed at women, whereas in men's magazines, it becomes vulgar, in the style of "Which Turkish bath?" You said jokingly that the first category belonged to the *scientia sexualis* and the second to an *ars erotica*; in any case, I see two things: on the one hand, the proliferation of *scientia sexualis* discourse, which is to say the overabundance of knowledge about sex, causing new frustration; and on the other hand, in our present circumstances, the *scientia sexualis* and *ars erotica* are difficult to distinguish from one another.

M. Foucault: Indeed, these sorts of functions are difficult to determine. In short, when scientific or even pseudo-scientific knowledge about sex is no longer provided only to doctors and sexologists but also to ordinary people and when the latter can apply this knowledge to their own sexual acts, the knowledge finds itself somewhere between an *ars erotica* and the *scientia sexualis*. This is the case of Reich and his supporters. According to them, if you really know your unconscious and your desire, you can reach orgasm, and this orgasm is good and must give you a lot of pleasure. In this case, the *scientia sexualis* is a rather rudimentary component of the *ars erotica*, rudimentary because orgasm is the only criterion.

M. Watanabe: What should be added is that in your analysis, the insertion of sex into discourse takes hold in the European tradition of avowal, which begins with Catholic confession and ends in psychoanalysis; it is indivisibly linked to a technique of Christian power, which you called the "morphological power of the priest" in today's lecture. The responsibility for the salvation of souls that the pastor-shepherd assumes for his believer-flock of sheep is a total understanding of all that goes on inside each believer in order that the subject and subjectivity be established in the Western world. In Japan, which modernized following the model of European society in the 19th century, this question of the subject was the most important philosophically and ethically, and many Japanese must be embarrassed that the formation of the subject-individual came from the point of view and through the technique of power that you described today in the lecture. Leaving this problem aside, you yourself have indicated that neither Buddhism nor Shintoism has understood humanity in this way, and I think the question is more complex.

M. Foucault: Certainly. What surprises Europeans who come to Japan is that Japan has perfectly assimilated the technology of the modem Western world; therefore, nothing is changed compared to the society they come from. And yet, on a human level, the mentality and the human relationships are very different. Here, the way of thinking prior to modernization and that of modern Europe coexist, and I intend to work on the analysis of these questions with Japanese specialists.

M. Watanabe: In *The Will to Knowledge*, you wrote that it is in "the body and pleasure" that one could find a support, perhaps antagonistic, with regard to sex as the incarnation of desire. But the body itself is ambiguous and can be thought of as an apparatus that is itself traversed by power.

M. Foucault: It is difficult to answer this question, because even for myself it isn't yet quite clear, but I think I can say this: the slogan launched by the sexual liberation movements, which is "liberate desire", strikes me not only as lacking persuasiveness but also as a bit dangerous. For this desire that is required, liberation is in fact only one constitutive part of sexuality, and is nothing more than what has been differentiated from the rest as carnal desires by the discipline of the Catholic Church and the technique of the examination of conscience. That is how, since the Middle Ages, we started to analyze desire in the Christian world, believing that it is precisely in desire that we can find the beginning of sin, and that we can see how it operates not only in sexual acts but in all areas of human behavior. Desire was thus a foundational element of sin. And liberating desire is nothing other than deciphering one's own unconscious, as psychoanalysts do, and long before them, the discipline of the Catholic confession made it a practice. The thing that is not talked about from this perspective is pleasure.

In this sense, I wrote that, if we wanted freedom from the science of sex, we had to find it in a foundation of pleasure, in the maximization of pleasure.

W. Watanabe: I hear that you were drawn to a Zen Buddhist temple. Was it to verify in person that the meaning of the body is different in Zen practices?

M. Foucault: Of course. The attitudes toward the body are very different in Zen and in Christianity, though both are religious practices. In the Christian practice of confession, the body is the object of an examination. We examine it in order to find out what indecent things are festering or manifesting. In this sense, in the discipline of confession, the way of examining the problem of masturbation is very interesting. It is certainly about the body, but seen as the principle of movements that influence the soul by taking the form of desire. Desire is suspected, and therefore the body becomes the problem.

But Zen is a totally different religious exercise in which the body is thought of as a kind of instrument. In this practice, the body serves as a support, and if the body is subjected to strict rules, it is in order to attain something through it.

C. Nemoto: I went to France last March to gather information on the general elections. I was struck by the unexpected failure of the Left. Listening to your lecture, I got the impression that you valued the new type of everyday battles led by citizens more than the electoral campaigns of existing political parties and you seemed to think that the result of the election is not very important.

M. Foucault: No, I did not speak at all about my position or my opinion on this subject. I did not say that the result was not important, but what surprised me a lot was, firstly, the stance of the majority as well as the opposition parties, which was to dramatize the situation. Second, we have never seen so many votes. But this very high percentage of votes does not mean, in itself, that the situation was dramatic in the mind of the voters. They voted because it is a civic duty to vote, but they did not seem passionate about the general election. In the electoral campaign, it was feared that there would be many abstentions, because the Right as well as the Left were only doing things that only warranted the indifference of voters. In the course of this campaign, there were a few TV shows or publications that had a strong impact on people. It wasn't Chirac's speech nor Mitterrand's, but those that dealt with the problem of death, the problem of the power that today's medical institutions exercise over our bodies, our life and our death. Obviously, the problem of death evokes a personal, emotional response for everyone. But, in this case, it was also accepted as a social problem. In short, it is a refusal of a medical right that makes decisions about our death without taking our intention into account. It is not the fear of medical ignorance, it is, on the contrary, a fear of medical knowledge. We fear that there is a link between this knowledge and an excess of power.

C. Nemoto: The new form of struggle that you mentioned in your lecture, the direct, struggle against everyday power, doesn't take into consideration political power on the national level or economic mechanisms; it reflects self-governance, ecology or feminist movements. It seems to me that these movements ended up being crushed in the general elections.

M. Foucault: This point reveals something very interesting. In the past, political parties were very interested in the percentage of votes that the ecologists would get, because in the district elections last year they reached 10 percent of the vote in some regions. What was surprising is that in the elections this time around, the ecologists scored as low as the feminist party. I don't think this phenomenon is a setback, because people knew very well that the method as well as the goal of day-to-day power struggles is different from what the general elections were about, where the focus is on centralized power. I don't think the environmental movements will be weakened by their failure in the last election; of course, this is an assumption.

C. Nemoto: So, these struggles don't have as their ultimate goal gaining power at the national level?

M. Foucault: No, as the everyday struggle against power doesn't aim to seize power—it in fact refuses it—power at the national level is not its object.

C. Nemoto: But aren't struggles of this type used and eventually hijacked by parties or political movements, at which point they lose their bite?

M. Foucault: If political parties and movements are interested in these struggles, that is proof that they are important. It's just a fact that there is always a risk of being taken over by the existing system.

But what does it mean to be taken over? It's normal to be wary of being taken over by the established system of management and control. I don't know about Japan, but in Europe the so-called far-left parties have what you might call a "propensity to fail".

C. Nemoto: It's the same in Japan.

M. Foucault: As soon as something succeeds and is realized, they claim that it has been taken over by the established regime! In short, they put themselves in the position of never being taken over, in other words, they are always obliged to suffer from failure. For example, in France, between 1972 and 1974, there were movements concerned with prisons. When Giscard d'Estaing was elected president and formed his first government, he carried out many new reforms. In particular, he created the role of Undersecretary of State at the Ministry of Justice, which was devoted exclusively to the problems of prison, and he appointed a woman.

So right away, die-hard leftists criticized: "Look! It's been taken over by the system!" But I don't think so.

This proves that this problem had been recognized as important at some level in the government's imaginary.

One difference between revolutionary movements and everyday struggles against power is precisely that the former do not want to succeed. What does succeed mean? It means that a request, any request, a strike for example, is accepted. But if the request is accepted, it proves that the capitalist adversaries remain very flexible, have various strategies and are able to survive. Revolutionary movements don't want this. Secondly, in accordance with a tactical vision already offered by Marx himself, there is the idea that revolutionary force is all the more important as discontent increases. If the request is accepted, that is to say if one succeeds, it implies that the revolutionary potentiality diminishes. All of the movements of the extreme left, from the years 1967 to 1972 in France, followed this pattern.

In short, everything is done to never succeed. The theory is that if one person is arrested, there would be ten protestors, if five people were arrested, there would be 300 protestors, and in this way, one could end up mobilizing 500,000 people. But everyone knows this led to a disastrous result.

On the other hand, the daily struggle against everyday power aims to succeed. They really believe they are winning. If they think that the construction of an airfield or a power plant at such and such a location is troublesome, they block it to the end. They aren't satisfied with a success as do the extreme left of revolutionary movements who think: "Our movements have moved two steps forward, but the revolution moved one step back". Success is success.

M. Watanabe: Mr. Foucault, you yourself took part in the movement Group for Information on Prisons; what will the role of intellectuals be in this regard?

M. Foucault: Nowadays, one can think that most of the manifestations of power against which the individual resists are diffused through channels of knowledge. The knowledge in question here is not limited to the knowledge of science, it is knowledge in the broad sense which includes all specialized knowledge such as that of technology and technocrats. For example, at the time of the absolute monarchy, there were farmers ensuring a public function that financed the king, who, in return, allowed them to collect the maximum amount of taxes from the population. People couldn't stand it and revolted against this way of doing things, much in the style of gangsters today.

The mechanism of power nowadays no longer follows this example of the gangster. It requires an enormous network of knowledge not only to function, but also to hide behind. Let's take the example of the hospital: the medical treatments themselves are certainly improving, but at the same time, medical power is reinforced and becomes more arbitrary. So, the resistance of intellectuals against this kind of power cannot overlook medicine nor the knowledge of medical treatment. On the contrary, in every discipline, whether medical or legal, insofar as they are linked to a network of knowledge and power, intellectuals can play the important role of providing and disseminating information that has remained confidential, specialized knowledge.

This change occurred between the '50s and '60s; previously, the role that intellectuals had played was to be a universal conscience.

C. Nemoto: Isn't that the case with Sartre?

M. Foucault: I don't wish to criticize Sartre. It is rather Zola who exemplifies this. He did not write Germinal (1885) as a minor.

All in all, with regard to the current struggle against everyday power, the possibility for intellectuals to be able to play a role and to make themselves useful exists in their specialization, but not in their universal consciousness.

What is important and interesting here is that, if one thinks in this way, the very framework of the intellectual suddenly widens. It is no longer necessary to be a universal philosopher and writer, as was previously the case for the universal intellectual. Everyone, whether a lawyer or a psychiatrist, can resist the use of power linked to the knowledge we have spoken about and contribute to preventing its implementation.

M. Watanabe: Such is the role of the intellectual that you call the specific intellectual.

Translated by Alice Mahoney

3

DISCIPLINARY SOCIETY IN CRISIS

"La société disciplinaire en crise", Conference at the Franco-Japanese Institute of Kansai, in Kyoto, April 18, 1978, in Asahi Jānaru, v. 20 no. 19, May 12, 1978.

Dits et écrits III, no. 231

What is the relationship between the classical theory of power and yours? And what is new in your theory?

It is not the theory that is different, but the object, the point of view. In general, the theory of power speaks of power in terms of rights and raises the question of its legitimacy, its limit and its origin. My research focuses on the techniques of power, on the technology of power. It consists in studying how power dominates and commands obedience. Since the 17th and 18th centuries, this technology has developed enormously; however, no research has been carried out. In today's society, various forms of resistance—such as feminism and student movements—have been born, and the relationship between these resistances and techniques of power constitutes an interesting subject of research.

DOI: 10.4324/9781003303763-5

It is the French society that is the subject of your analyses? To what extent could these results be applied universally? For example, are they directly applicable to Japanese society? This is an important question. The object of the analysis is always determined by time and space, although we try to give it universality. My aim is to analyze the technique of power—which always seeks new means—and my object is a society subject to criminal legislation. This society differs in France, Germany, and Italy. There is a difference of systems. However, the mechanisms that make power effective are shared. Accordingly, I have chosen France as an example of a European society subject to criminal legislation. I looked at how discipline has developed there, how it changed with the development of industrial society and an increase in population. Discipline, which was once so effective in maintaining power, has lost some of its effectiveness. In industrialized countries, discipline is in crisis.

You have just spoken of "discipline crises". What will happen after these crises? Is a new society possible?

For four to five centuries, it has been considered that the development of Western society depended on the effectiveness of power in fulfilling its role. For example, it mattered in the family how the authority of the father or the parents controlled the behavior of the children. If this mechanism broke, society would collapse. How the individual obeyed was the important subject. In recent years, society has changed and so have individuals; they are increasingly diverse, different, and independent. There are more and more categories of people who are not subject to discipline, so we are forced to think about the development of a society without discipline. The ruling class is still steeped in the older approach. But it is obvious that we must separate ourselves in the future from the disciplined society of today.

You emphasize the importance of micro-powers, whereas, in today's world, state power is still the main theme. Where is public power situated in your theory of power?

In general, the preference is for state power. Many people think that other forms of power derive themselves from it. But I think that, without going so far as to say that state power derives from other forms of power, it is at least based on them, and it is they that allow state power to exist. How can we say that all the power relations that exist derive from state power? Between the two sexes, between adults and children, in the family, in offices, between the sick and the healthy, between normal and abnormal? If we want to change state power, we have to change the various power relations that function in society. Otherwise, society does not change. For example, in the USSR the ruling class changed but the old power relations remained. What is important is the power relations that operate independently of the individuals who have state power.

In Discipline and Punish, you write that power changes and knowledge changes. Is this a pessimistic perspective of knowledge?

I did not say that the two categorically depend on one another. Since Plato, we've known that knowledge cannot exist totally independent of power. This does not mean that knowledge is subject to political power, because quality knowledge cannot be born under such conditions. But the development of scientific knowledge is impossible to understand without taking into account the changes in the mechanisms of power. The best example would be that of economic sciences. But also, a science like biology has evolved according to complex elements, such as developments in agriculture, relations with foreign countries, or the domination of colonies. We cannot think about the progress of scientific knowledge without thinking about mechanisms of power.

As a concrete case concerning knowledge and power, I am afraid that my question is indiscreet; you approach research on power in a radical and critical way and you came to Japan as a cultural delegate of the French government. This would not happen easily in Japan.

France is passionate about exporting its culture and would even export a toxic substance if it were a French product. Japan is a relatively free country, and my works are freely translated there; therefore, it is now useless to prohibit me from going to Japan. Throughout the world, cultural exchanges have become frequent and important, and it is impossible to prohibit the release of ideas abroad, unless a regime is absolutely dictatorial. I don't think at all that the French government is a completely liberal government, but one could say that it recognizes reality as it is and it does not prohibit it.

Translated by Alice Mahoney

4

THE ANALYTIC PHILOSOPHY OF POWER

"Gendai no Kenryoku wo tou" (*"La philosophie analytique de la politique"*); lecture delivered on April 2, 1978, at the Asahi Kodo conference center in Tokyo and office of the journal, in Asahi Jānaru, June 2, 1978, pp. 28–35.

Dits et écrits III, no. 232

I had proposed, among possible topics for this lecture, a talk about prisons, about the specific problem of prisons. I have come to give up that topic for several reasons: the first being that, after three weeks in Japan, I have noticed that the problem of penality—of criminality, of the prison—is set up in your society in very different terms than it is in ours. I have perceived likewise, in having been to a prison—when I say that I have been to a prison, that does not mean that I was confined in one, but that I visited a prison, two even, in the Fukuoka region—that, in relation to what we know in Europe, this prison did not represent just an instantiation, an advancement, but a veritable mutation that makes it necessary that there be reflection and discussion of the

DOI: 10.4324/9781003303763-6

question with Japanese specialists. I felt ill at ease in speaking to you about problems the way they are currently posed in Europe, when you have experiences that are so important. And, finally, the problem of prisons is, in sum, but one part, one piece in a greater whole of more general problems. The conversations I have been able to have with various Japanese people have convinced me that it would be of greater interest to evoke not only the general climate in which the question of the prison, of penality, has its position, but also a certain number of topical questions of pressing and urgent actuality. Taking this into account, I ask your pardon for giving this talk a bit more generality than would be limited to the problem of the prison. If you should have any objection, you can address it with me.

You know no doubt that there is a journal in France called *Le Monde*, which one habitually refers to, with a great deal of solemnity, as a "great evening newspaper". In this "great evening newspaper", a journalist had written one day the following, which amazed me and which I bring myself to consider. "Why", he wrote, "do so many people today engage with the question of power? Someday", he continued, "it will no doubt be surprising how forcefully vexing this question of power was to us at the end of the 20th century".

I do not believe that our successors, if they would reflect just a bit more, would remain surprised for long that, precisely at the end of the 20th century, people of our generation would have dealt so insistently with the question of power. Because, after all, if the question of power is posed, it is not at all because we have posed it. It poses itself, it was posed to us. It was posed to us by current events, that is for sure, but also by our past, by an all-too-recent past that is barely over. After all, the 20th century knew two great diseases of power, two great fevers that carried far and wide the aggravated symptoms of a kind of power. These two great diseases, which dominated the core, the very environment, of the 20th century, are, of course, fascism and Stalinism. Of course, fascism and Stalinism each responded to a very precise and specific historical conjuncture. Without a doubt, fascism and Stalinism drove their effects to dimensions hitherto unknown that one can hope, if not reasonably think, will never be known again.

They are thus singular phenomena; yet it cannot be denied that, by and large, fascism and Stalinism only prolonged a series of mechanisms that already existed in the social and political systems of the West. After all, the organization of the major parties, the development of policing apparatuses, the existence of techniques of repression like work camps, are all well part of a legacy of Western liberal societies that Stalinism and fascism did nothing but inherit.

It is this experience that has obligated us to deal with the question of power. For one cannot avoid asking and interrogating oneself: were fascism and Stalinism, and, where they still persist, are they, merely the response to historical conjunctures and particular situations? Or, on the contrary, do we need to consider that there may exist in our societies lasting potentialities, somehow structural, intrinsic to our systems, that may reveal themselves at every turn, rendering perpetually possible these sorts of gross excrescences of power, these excrescences for which the Mussolinian, Hitlerian, and Stalinist systems, the current system in Chile, the current system in Cambodia, serve as examples, and inevitable examples at that?

The major problem, I believe, of the 19th century, in Europe at least, was that of poverty and misery. The major problem that presented itself to most thinkers and philosophers at the beginning of the 19th century was: how is it that the production of wealth, whose spectacular effects began to be recognized throughout the West, how is it that this production of wealth could be accompanied by impoverishment—either in absolute or relative terms (itself another question)—by the impoverishment indeed of the very ones who produced this wealth? This problem of the impoverishment of the ones who produce the wealth, the problem of the simultaneous production of wealth and poverty, I do not say that it has been completely resolved in the West at the end of the 20th century, but that it no longer presents itself with the same urgency. It finds itself redoubled by another problem, which is no longer one of too much wealth but one of too much power. Western societies and, in general, industrialized and developed societies at the end of this century, are societies that are crisscrossed by this dull disquiet, if not by movements of revolt that overtly put into question this type of overproduction of power that Stalinism and fascism manifested beyond doubt in its naked and monstrous state. Hence, just as the 19th century needed an economy that had the production and distribution of wealth as its specific goal, one could say that we need an economy that is not focused on the production and distribution of wealth but an economy that addresses relations of power.

One of the oldest functions of the philosopher in the West—"the philosopher", I could also say "sage" or maybe, to use this ugly contemporary word, "intellectual"—one of the principal roles of the philosopher in the West has been to set a limit, to set a limit to the excess of power, to this overproduction of power every time and in all cases when it risks becoming a threat. The philosopher in the West has always had, more or less, the profile of an anti-despot. And that profile has emerged in several possible forms since the beginning of Greek philosophy.

The philosopher has been anti-despotic in defining the system of laws according to which power had to be exercised in a city, in defining the legal limits within which it could be wielded without danger: this is the role of the philosopher-legislator. This was Solon's role. After all, the moment when Greek philosophy began to separate itself from poetry, the moment when Greek prose began to emerge, was well likely the day when Solon formulated, in a vocabulary that was still poetic, the laws that would become the very prose of Greek history, of Hellenic history.

The second possibility: the philosopher can be anti-despotic in making himself the counselor of the prince, in teaching him this wisdom, that virtue, or that truth that would have the capacity to keep him, when it is his turn to govern, from abusing his power. This is the philosopher-pedagogue: it is Plato making his pilgrimage to Dionysius of Syracuse.

Finally, the third possibility: the philosopher can be anti-despotic in saying that, after all, whatever abuses power may level at him or at others, the philosopher, insofar as he is a philosopher, remains, both in his philosophical practice as in his philosophical thought, independent in relation to power. He laughs at power. This would be the position of the cynics.

Solon the legislator, Plato the pedagogue, and the cynics. The philosopher as regulator of power, the philosopher as mask grimacing in the face of power. If we take an ethnological look at the West since Greece, we would see these three figures of the philosopher taking turns, replacing one other; one would see a relationship of significant opposition emerging between the philosopher and the prince, between philosophical reflection and the exercise of power. And I wonder whether this opposition between philosophical reflection and the exercise of power may characterize philosophy better than its relation to science, since, after all, it has been long since that philosophy has played the role of foundation in relation to science. However, the role of moderation or regulation in relation to power is one that may deserve still to be played.

When one looks at the manner in which, historically, the philosopher has played or been interested in playing the role of regulator of power, one arrives at a conclusion with a slightly bitter aftertaste. Antiquity has seen philosopher-legislators; it has seen philosophers who have served as counselors to princes; yet, there has never been, as an example, a Platonic city. Alexander may have been Aristotle's disciple, but Alexander's empire was not Aristotelian. And, if it is true that, in the Roman Empire, Stoicism imbued the thought of the entire world, at least of the elite, it is no less true that the Roman Empire was not Stoic. Stoicism was for Marcus Aurelius a way of being emperor; it was neither an art nor a technique of governing the empire.

In other words—and here I think is an important point regarding the difference of what has happened in the East, particularly in China and Japan—there has not been in the West, at least not for a very long time, a philosophy that has been able to be joined to a political practice, a moral practice of an entire society. The West has never known the equivalent of Confucianism, that is to say, a form of thought that, in reflecting the order of the world, or, in establishing it, prescribes at the same time the structure of the State, the form of social relations, of individual conduct, and does so within the very reality of history. However important Aristotelian thought has been, as favored as Aristotelianism was by the dogmatism of the Middle Ages, never has

Aristotle played a role comparable to that played by Confucius in the East. There has not been a philosophical State in the West.

But things changed—and here I think an important event is marked—starting from the French Revolution, starting from the end of the 18th century and the beginning of the 19th. One sees then the formation of political regimes with ties or links to philosophies that are not simply ideological but organic, I would say "organizational". The French Revolution, one may even say the Napoleonic Empire, had with Rousseau, but, more generally speaking, with philosophy of the 18th century, organic ties. An organic link between the Prussian State and Hegel; an organic link, as paradoxical as it may be—but that is another matter—between the Hitlerian State and Wagner and Nietzsche. Links, of course, between Leninism, the Soviet State, and Marx. The 19th century saw appear in Europe something that had never existed until then: philosophical States, I might say "philosophy-States", philosophies that are at the same time States, and States that think, reflect, organize themselves, and define their fundamental choices by proceeding from philosophical propositions, from inside philosophical systems, as the philosophical truth of history. There one sees a phenomenon that is evidently quite astonishing and that becomes more troubling as one reflects on how these philosophies, all these philosophies that have become States, have been without exception philosophies of liberty— philosophies of liberty of the 18th century, of course, but philosophies of liberty as well in Hegel, Nietzsche, and Marx. These philosophies of liberty gave rise each time to forms of power—be it in the form of terror, in the form of bureaucracy, or in the form of bureaucratic terror—that were the very opposite of the regime of liberty, the very opposite of liberty become history.

There is a bitter irony about these modern Western philosophers: they thought, and they thought of themselves, in terms of an essentially oppositional relationship to power and its unlimited exercise, but the trajectory of their thought made it such that the more they were listened to, the more power and political institutions became imbued with their thought, the more they themselves served to authorize excessive forms of power. This was, after all, the sad comedy of Hegel transformed into the Bismarckian regime; this was the sadly comic fate of Nietzsche, whose complete works were given by Hitler to Mussolini on the trip to Venice to sanction the Anschluss. More even than the dogmatic endorsements of religions, philosophy gives authorization to unbridled powers. This paradox reached acute crisis with Stalinism, which presented itself as a State that was, more than any other, at the same time a philosophy, a philosophy that had announced and predicted the very withering away of the State itself and that, transformed into the State, had become a veritably private State, cut off from all philosophical reflection and possibility of reflection by any means. This is the philosophical State having become literally unconscious in the form of the pure State.

In the face of this situation that is very precisely and so pressingly contemporary for us, there are several possible attitudes. One may, it is perfectly legitimate, I would even say advisable, conduct a historical interrogation of the strange links that the West has forged or allowed to be forged between philosophers and power: how is it that these links between philosophy and power could be formed at the very moment when philosophy gave itself as principle, if not the function of counter-power, at least that of the moderation of power, at the moment when philosophy should have said to power: "There will you stop yourself, and there you will go no further"? Is it a question of a betrayal of philosophy? Or is it because philosophy has always been secretly, regardless of what is said, a certain philosophy of power? Or is the very act of saying to power, "Stop there, you!", not precisely, virtually, and secretly, one that assumes the place of power, that lays down the law of the law, and therefore realizes itself as law?

One may raise all these questions. One can, on the contrary, say to oneself that philosophy has nothing to do with power, that the profound and essential vocation of philosophy is to deal with truth or to interrogate being; and that philosophy can only compromise itself by straying in empirical domains after the question of politics and power. If philosophy is so easily betrayed, it is because philosophy has already betrayed itself. Philosophy has betrayed itself by going where philosophy ought not to have gone, by posing questions that were not philosophy's to pose.

But maybe there is yet another way. It is about this way that I would like to speak to you. Perhaps one can still conceive for philosophy the possibility of playing a role in relation to power that would not be foundational or contractually renewable. Perhaps philosophy can still play a role on the side of counter-power, on the condition that this role no longer consist of affirming, in the face of power, the law of philosophy itself; on the condition that philosophy cease to think of itself as prophecy; on the condition that philosophy cease to think of itself as either pedagogy or legislation—but that philosophy should give itself the task of analyzing, elucidating, making visible, and thus intensifying the struggles that unfold around power, the strategies of adversaries within relations of power, the tactics used, the vestibulary sites of resistance—on the condition, in sum, that philosophy cease to raise the question of power in terms of good or bad, but in terms of existence. Not to ask: is power good or is it bad, legitimate or illegitimate, a question of right or of morality? But, simply, to try to relieve the question of power of all the moral and juridical excess that has been assigned it up to this point, and to pose the following naive question, which has not been raised very often, even if a certain number of people have, in effect, been asking it for a long time: what, in fact, are relations of power made of?

It has been quite a while since one has known that the role of philosophy is not to discover what is hidden but to render visible precisely what is visible, that is to say, to make appear that which is near, that which is immediate, that which is intimately connected to us and, for that reason, unperceived by us. While the role of science is to make known what we do not see, the role of philosophy is to make us see what we do see. All things considered, the task of philosophy today could well be: what are these relations of power in which we are caught and in which philosophy itself, for at least 150 years, has been entangled?

You will tell me that this task is fairly modest, quite empirical, fairly limited, but one finds nearby enough the model of a similar use of philosophy in Anglo-American analytic philosophy. After all, Anglo-Saxon analytic philosophy does not see its task as reflecting on the being of language or the profound structures of language; it reflects on the everyday use one makes of language in different types of discourse. For Anglo-Saxon analytic philosophy, the concern is to perform a critical analysis of thought proceeding from the manner in which one says things. I believe that one could imagine, in the same way, a philosophy that would have as its task analyzing what takes place on a quotidian level in relations of power, a philosophy that would try to show how things work, what are the forms, stakes, and objectives in these relations of power. A philosophy that would thus be about relations of power rather than games of language, a philosophy that would be about all the relations that traverse the social body rather than the effects of language that traverse and subtend thought. One could imagine—one would have to imagine—something like an analytic-political philosophy. One would then have to recall that Anglo-Saxon analytic philosophy of language amasses species of linguistic qualifications and disqualifications like what one finds in Humboldt or Bergson—in Humboldt, for whom language was the creator of all possible relations between man and the world, the very creator, indeed, of the world inasmuch as the human being; or in the Bergsonian devalorization that does not cease to repeat that language is impotent, that language is frozen, that language is dead, that language is spatio-structural, such that one cannot but betray the experience of consciousness and duration. Instead of these massive disqualifications or qualifications, Anglo-Saxon philosophy tries to say that language neither deceives nor reveals entirely. Language plays. The importance, therefore, of the notion of play.

One could say, in a somewhat analogous fashion, that to analyze or critique relations of power is not to assign qualifying terms either pejorative or laudatory in nature that would be massified, global, definitive, absolute, and unilateral in scope; it is not about saying that relations of power can do only one thing, which is constrain or coerce. One must no longer imagine that one can escape from relations of power once and for all, on a global and massive scale, through a sort of radical rupture or a flight without return. Language, like relations of power, is at play as well. These are games of power that must be studied in terms of tactic and strategy, in terms of rule and risk, in terms of stake and objective. It is somewhat along these lines that I have tried to work and that I would like to indicate to you a few lines of analysis that may be pursued.

These games of power can be approached from a good number of angles. Rather than studying the great game played between the State and citizens or between the State and other States, I have preferred—no doubt due to a tendency in my own character or a personal neurotic obsession—to interest myself in games of power that are far more limited and far more humble, games that do not have the elevated, recognized status of the big problems: games of power around madness; games of power around medicine, around illness, around the diseased body; games of power around penality and the prison. This has, somehow or other, maintained my interest up to the present moment, and for two reasons.

What is in question in these games of power, which are tenuous, somewhat aberrant, sometimes marginal? Implicated in them are nothing more and nothing less than the status of reason and non-reason, the status of life and death, the status of criminality and legality: that is to say, the whole of things that constitute the weave of our everyday lives and on which humans have constructed their discourse of tragedy.

There is another reason why I have interested myself in these questions and games of power. It seems to me that these games, more than great State and institutional battles, carry the weight of the worry and interest of people in our days. When one sees, for example, the way legislative electoral campaigns unroll in France, one is struck by how the newspapers, the media, the politicians, and those in positions of responsibility in government and in the State do not cease repeating to the French how they are in the process of playing a leading role for the future, whatever the result of the elections will have been, whatever the number of wise voters will have shown up to vote. One is struck by the fact how people have absolutely not felt, on a deep level, what could be historically tragic or decisive in these elections.

What has struck me, on the contrary, over the years is the uninterrupted whirring, not only in French society but in many societies, over questions that have been at other times marginal or a little too theoretical: knowing how to die, knowing what will be done to you when you find yourself confused in a hospital, knowing what your sanity is and the judgment others make of your sanity, knowing what it is to be mad, knowing what committing an infraction would be and what would happen when one commits an infraction or begins to enter the machinery of penality. All this touches closely upon the life, the affectivity, and the pain of our contemporaries. If you tell me, rightly, that things have, after all, always been this way, it still seems to me that this is one of the first times (if not altogether the first time). In one way or another, we are at one of those moments when these quotidian questions, marginal and remaining somewhat muffled, accede to an explicit level of discourse, where people accept not only to speak of them, but to enter the game of discourse and take a side in it. Madness and reason, death and sickness, penality, the prison, crime, the law: all these form our everyday, and this everyday is what appears to us as essential.

I think, moreover, that one must go further and say that not only have these games of power around life and death, reason and unreason, law and criminality, taken on an intensity that they did not have in the least in the immediately preceding period, but that the resistance and struggles that unfold no longer have the same form. It is no longer essential to take part in these games of power for the betterment of personal liberty or rights; one is simply no longer interested in these games. What matters is no longer confrontations within the limits of the games, but resistance to the game and refusal of the game itself. This characterizes, on the whole, a certain number of struggles and fights.

Take the case of the prison. For years and years, one could say for centuries, in any case since the existence of the prison as a type of punishment within Western penal systems, a whole series of movements, critiques, and sometimes violent opposition developed since the 19th century in attempts to modify the function of the prison, the condition of the prisoner, their status, be it in prison or afterward. We know that now, and for the first time, it is no longer about this game or that resistance, about a particular position within the game; it is about, rather, a refusal of the game itself. What one says is: no more prison at all. And then, in response to this type of wholesale critique, the reasonable people, legislators, technocrats, and persons in charge ask, "But what then do you want?" The response is: "It is not up to us to tell you what tomorrow will bring; we are not interested in this game of penality any longer; we do not want to play this game of penal sanctions any more; we do not want to play this game of justice any more". It seems telling to me that, in the history of Narita that has unfolded over the years in Japan, the game of the adversaries and those who resist has not been to obtain as many advantages as possible, by validating the law, by obtaining indemnities. One has not wanted to play the game, as it is traditionally organized and institutionalized by the State with its requirements and citizens with their rights. There has been no interest in playing the game at all: the game is kept from being played.

The second characteristic of these phenomena that I am attempting to locate and analyze is their diffuse and decentered form. Here is what I mean. Let us take again the example of the prison and the penal system. In the 18th century, in the 1760s, the epoch when a radical change of the penal system was first proposed, who was it who posed the question, and from what point of departure? It was the doing of theorists, theorists of rights, philosophers of the epoch, for whom the problem was not prison itself at all, but the very general problem of what law should be in a country of liberty and how the law should be applied, within which parameters and up to what limit. It is as a consequence of this central theoretical reflection that, after a certain number of years, prison emerged as the apt punishment, as the only possible punishment.

The problem has posed itself in entirely different terms, and in an altogether different way, in recent years in Western countries. The point of departure was never a grand, global claim concerning a better system of law. The points of departure were always trivial and miniscule: stories of malnutrition and discomfort in prisons. And, from these local phenomena, from these very particular points of departure, in these specific sites, one noticed that the phenomenon diffused, spreading very quickly and implicating a whole file of people who were never in the same situation or had the same problems. One may add that these instances of resistance seem relatively indifferent to political regimes and economic systems, sometimes even to the social structures of the countries where they develop. One saw, for example, struggles, resistances, and strikes in prisons in Sweden, whose penal system and penitentiary system are extremely progressive in relation to ours, just as in countries like Italy or Spain, where the situation was quite bad and the political context entirely different.

One could say the same thing about the women's movement and struggles around games of power between men and women. The feminist movement developed in Sweden as well as in Italy, where the status of women, the status of sexual relations, and relations between man and wife, men and women, were so different. This shows well that the goal of all these movements is not the same as that of traditional political and revolutionary movements: they are absolutely not aimed at political power or the economic system.

Third characteristic: this type of resistance and struggle targets essentially the facts of power themselves, much more than something like economic exploitation, much more than something like a disparity. What is in question in these struggles is the fact of a certain exercise of power, with the very fact of its exercise being unacceptable. I will give an anecdote for example, which you can smile about, but which you can also take seriously: in Sweden, there are prisons where detainees can receive conjugal visits from their wives. Each detainee gets a room. One day, a young Swedish woman, a student and ardent militant, came to look for me to ask me to help denounce fascism in Swedish prisons. I asked her what this fascism consists of. She responded: the rooms in which prisoners receive conjugal visits do not have locks. Of course, that is cause for laughter; it is at the same time very significant that power is in question here.

In the same way, the series of reproaches and critiques that have been directed against the medical institution—I think of those of Illich but of many others as well—do not deal essentially, principally, with the fact that medical institutions function as profit-driven medicine, even if one can denounce the relations there may be between pharmaceutical companies and certain medical practices or hospital institutions. In finding fault with medicine, it is not so much that one does not make use of it but that medical knowledge is fragile and often erroneous. It is essentially, it seems to me, to exert uncontrolled power over the body, over the suffering of the sick, over the sick person's life and death. I don't know if it is the same thing in Japan, but in European countries, it strikes me that the problem of death is raised not as a reproach to medicine for being unable to keep us alive longer but, on the contrary, of keeping us alive even when we do not want it. We reproach medicine, medical knowledge, and the medical technostructure for making life and death decisions for us, for keeping us alive in a scientifically and technologically very sophisticated way, but in a way we no longer want. The right to death is the right to say no to medical knowledge, and it is not an exigency that medical knowledge should exercise. The target is power.

In the Narita affair, one finds also something like this: the farmers of Narita would certainly have gained non-negligible advantages by accepting certain of the proposals that were made to them. Their refusal was directed towards a form of power exercised on them that they were not interested in. Much more than the economic stake, it is the very modality of the power imposed on them, the very fact that it was an expropriation decided on high in a particular manner that was in play in the Narita affair: to such arbitrary power one responds with a violent inversion of power.

The last characteristic I would like to insist about these struggles is that they are immediate struggles. In two senses. In one sense, they take aim at the closest examples of power; they go after everything that has an immediate effect on individuals. In other words, these struggles are not about following the great Leninist principle of the main enemy or the weakest link. These immediate struggles no longer await a future moment that would be the revolution, that would be liberation, that would be the disappearance of classes, that would be the withering away of the State as the solution of problems. In relation to a theoretical hierarchy of explanations or a revolutionary order that would polarize history and hierarchize it into moments, one may say that these struggles are anarchic struggles; they inscribe themselves within a history that is immediate, that accepts and recognizes itself as indefinite and open.

I would like to return now to this analytic-political philosophy that I was just talking about. It seems to me that the role of such an analytic philosophy of power would have to gauge the importance of such struggles and such phenomena, to which only marginal value has been accorded until now. One would have to show how these processes, agitations, and struggles—often obscure, middling, small—how these struggles differ from the forms of struggle that were so strongly valorized in the West under the sign of revolution. It is absolutely evident that, whatever the vocabulary employed, whatever the theoretical references of those who participate in the struggles, what is in play is a process that, while being altogether important, is absolutely not a formal process of revolutionary morphology, in the classic sense of the word "revolution"—wherein "revolution" designates a global struggle involving nations, peoples, and classes as unitary entities; a struggle that promises to overturn established power from top to bottom, to annihilate its very principle; a struggle that guarantees total liberation; a struggle whose status as necessary demands, in the final count, that all other struggles be subordinate and suspended in relation to it.

Are we witnessing, at the end of the 20th century, something like the end of the age of revolution? This kind of prophecy, this kind of condemnation to death of revolution seems to be somewhat ridiculous. We are perhaps living the end of a historical period that, since 1789 to 1793, has been, at least in the West, dominated by the monopoly of revolution, in conjunction with all the effects of despotism that may be implicated, without this monopoly of revolution, however, signifying a revaluation of reformism. The struggles of which I have just spoken do not deal, in effect, with reformism at all, since the role of reformism is to stabilize a system of power towards the goal of making a number of changes, whereas all these struggles are about the destabilization of mechanisms of power, about a destabilization apparently without end.

Decentered in relation to principles, leaders, and privileges of revolution, these struggles are not, however, circumstantial phenomena linked only to particular historical conjunctures. They deal with a historical reality that has existed in a perhaps inapparent but extremely durable way in Western societies for centuries. It seems to me that these struggles deal with one of the lesser-known but essential structures of our societies. Certain forms of exercising power are perfectly visible and have engendered struggles that can be recognized right away, since their target is itself visible: against colonial, ethnic, linguistic forms of domination, there have been nationalist struggles, social struggles whose explicit and known target were economic forms of exploitation; there have been political struggles against well-known and visible juridical and political forms of power. The struggles I speak of—and this is perhaps why the analysis thereof demands more delicacy than that of the others—take aim at a power that has existed in the West since the Middle Ages, a form of power that is neither exactly political or juridical, nor economic, nor a power of ethnic domination, but that has great structuring effects within our societies. This power is a power of religious origin: it is that which claims to lead and direct men in a lifelong way and in every circumstance of life, a power that consists of the desire to take charge of the existence of men in detail and in its unfolding from birth till death, to constrain men to a way of comporting themselves for their salvation. This is what one may call pastoral power.

Etymologically, to take words entirely at face value, pastoral power is the power that the shepherd wields over his flock. A power of this kind, so attentive, so full of solicitude, so attached to the wellbeing of each and all, was unknown to and probably unsuitable for ancient societies, out of place in Greek and Roman societies. It was only with Christianity, with the institution of the Church and its hierarchical and territorial organization, along with the collection of beliefs regarding the afterlife, sin, salvation, the merit economy, and with the definition of the role of the priest, that there appeared the conception of Christians as members of a flock, over which a certain number of individuals, who enjoy a particular status, have the right and duty to carry out the offices of the pastorate.

Pastoral power developed throughout the Middle Ages in close and difficult relation to feudal society. It developed, even more intensely, in the 16th century, with the Reformation and the Counter-Reformation. Through this history that began with Christianity and continued until the heart of the classical age, till the very eve of the Revolution, pastoral power retained an essential, singular character in the history of civilizations: pastoral power, in being wielded like no other type of religious or political power over an entire group, had, as its principal task and concern, keeping watch over the wellbeing of all, taking charge of every particular element, every sheep of the flock, every individual, not just to constrain each one to act in such and such a way, but also to know, to discover, and to reveal the subjectivity thereof, and to structure the relation of each to himself and to his own conscience. The techniques of the Christian pastorate regarding the guidance of the conscience, the care for souls, the cure of souls; all these practices that are put to the test in the rite of confession—in one's obligatory relationship to oneself in terms of truth and required speech: these seem to me one of the fundamental points of pastoral power and what makes it an individualizing power. Power in Greek city-states and in the Roman Empire did not involve the need to know individuals one by one, to constitute in each individual a sort of small kernel of truth that confession must bring to light and that the attentive listening of the pastor must receive and judge. Feudal power no longer needed this individualizing economy of power. Absolute monarchy and its administrative apparatus likewise no longer needed it. These latter forms of power dealt with an entire society, groups, territories, or categories of individuals. One was a member of groups or ranks in these societies; one was not yet in an individualizing society. Well before the great epoch of the development of industrial and bourgeois society, the religious power of Christianity molded the social body to the point of constituting individuals linked to one another in the form of a subjectivity to which one demands self-consciousness in terms of truth and in the form of confession.

I would like to make two remarks regarding pastoral power. First, that it would be worthwhile to compare the pastorate, the pastoral power of Christian societies, with what would have been the role of effects of Confucianism in the societies of the Far East. One must remark upon the near chronological coincidence of the two, one must remark upon how the role of pastoral power was important in the development of the State from the 16th to the 17th century in Europe, somewhat like Confucianism was in Japan in the Tokugawa Period. But one must also differentiate between pastoral power and Confucianism: the pastorate is essentially religious, Confucianism is not; the pastorate shows essentially an aim situated in the beyond and that intervenes here below only in its function of indicating this beyond, while Confucianism plays an essentially terrestrial role; Confucianism aims for a general stability of the social body by means of a collection of general rules that are imposed on all individuals and all categories of individuals, while the pastorate establishes relationships of obedience that are individualized between the pastor and his flock; finally, the pastorate achieves individualizing effects that Confucianism does not through techniques such as spiritual guidance, care of souls, etc. There is an important world of studies that one can develop starting from fundamental work done in Japan by Masao Maruyama.

My second remark is this: that, in a paradoxical and insufficiently heeded manner, starting with the 18th century, capitalist and industrial societies, as much as the modern State forms that accompanied and supported them, needed procedures, mechanisms, essentially, procedures of individualization, that the religious pastorate had put into operation. Whatever leave or reprieve may have been given a certain number of religious institutions, whatever may have been the mutations that one calls, in short, "ideological"—which certainly profoundly modified the relationship of Western man to religious beliefs, there was the implantation, even multiplication and diffusion, of pastoral techniques in the lay cadre of the state apparatus. One knows little of it and one speaks little of it, no doubt because the great State forms that were developed since the 18th century were justified much more in terms of assurances of liberty than in terms of implanted mechanisms of power, and maybe also because these little mechanisms of power had something humble and unavowable that one did not think it necessary to analyze or say. As one writer puts it in a novel called *An Ordinary Man*, the established order prefers to ignore the mechanics that organize its so evidently tawdry functioning, such that the machinery ends up destroying all appeals for justice.

It is exactly these little mechanisms, humble and seemingly tawdry, that one must bring into relief against the backdrop of the society in which they function. During the European 18th and 19th centuries, one witnessed an entire reconversion, a thoroughgoing transplantation of what had been the traditional objectives of the pastorate. It is often said that the State and modern societies ignore the individual. When one takes a closer look, however, one is struck by the attention that the State brings to bear upon individuals; one is struck by all the techniques that have been put into place and developed so that the individual does not in any way escape power, surveillance, control, proper conduct, rectification, or correction. All the great disciplinary machines—barracks, schools, workshops, and prisons—are machines that make it possible to encircle the individual, to know where he is, what he does, what one can do with him, where he must be placed, how to place him among others. The human sciences are also ways of knowing that make it possible to know what are individuals, what is normal and what is not, what is reasonable and what is not, who is competent and to do what, which are foreseeable behaviors of individuals, which are ones that have to be eliminated. The importance of statistics derives exactly from the fact that statistics makes it possible to measure quantitatively the mass effects of individual behavior. One must add here that mechanisms of services and insurance, apart from their objectives of economic rationalization and political stabilization, have individualizing effects: they make the individual, his existence and behavior, his life—the existence of not only all but each—an event that is relevant, even necessary and indispensable, to the exercise of power in modern societies. The individual has become a stake essential to the play of power. Power grew all the more individualizing, paradoxically, the more bureaucratic and statist it became. If the pastorate lost, in its strictly religious form, the essential core of its power, it found in the State a new base and a principle of transformation.

I would like to end by returning to those struggles, to those games of power of which I spoke earlier and of which the struggles around the prison and the penal system are only one example and one possible case. These struggles—be they those about madness, mental illness, reason and unreason; be they those about sexual relations between individuals or relations between the sexes; be they about the environment and what one calls "ecology"; be they ones that deal with medicine, health, and death—these struggles have a goal and a very precise stake that gives them importance, a stake altogether different from the aims involved in revolutionary struggles and that deserves to be taken at least as much into consideration. That which one hails, since the 19th century, as the Revolution, that which the parties and so-called revolutionary movements aim for, is essentially what constitutes economic power.

Translated by Emily Sun

5

SEXUALITY AND POWER

"Sei to kenryoku" ("Sexuality and Power"), conference in Tokyo on April 20, 1978, followed by a debate, in Gendai-shisō, July 1978, pp. 58–77.

Dits et écrits III, no. 233

First of all, I would like to thank those in charge at the University in Tokyo for allowing me to come here and have this meeting with you. I would have preferred a seminar during which each and every one of us would be able to discuss, ask questions, and try to answer them; but more often than not, ask questions rather than answer them. I'd especially like to thank Mr. Watanabe. Over the years, he has kindly met with me every time he came to France, took such paternal—or maternal—care of me when I was in Japan, and I really don't know how to express my gratitude for what he has done and what he still does now.

This afternoon, I thought we would have the opportunity to discuss, in a small group, around a table which we call round, even if it is sometimes square; I mean around a table that would allow for equal and continual exchanges. The large number of participants—for which I am grateful, of course, has the inconvenience of forcing me

DOI: 10.4324/9781003303763-7

to take on this position of master, this position of distance, and also obliges me to speak in a way that will be a little bit continuous, even if I try to make it as undogmatic as possible. Anyways, I would like to communicate neither a theory, nor a doctrine, not even the result of a research, because as Mr. Watanabe recalled, I had the opportunity to see that most of my books and articles are translated into Japanese. It would also be indecent and rude on my part to go over them again and to impose them as dogma. I would rather explain where I am now and what kinds of problems I am dealing with and submit to you some of the hypotheses that underlie my current work. Of course, I would be very happy if after this presentation, which I hope will last half an hour or 45 minutes, we can have a discussion, and maybe at that point, the atmosphere will be—how shall I say—more relaxed, and it will be easier to exchange questions and answers. It goes without saying of course that you can ask questions in Japanese—I will not understand them, but they will be translated for me; you can also ask questions in English. I will answer in a babble of sorts and there again we will find a way. I will try—since you have had the kindness to attend a lecture in French—to speak as clearly as possible. I know, given the professors you have, that I don't have to worry about your linguistic ability, but still, proper etiquette requires that I try to make myself understood, so, if you have any problems or difficulties, or if you do not understand, or simply if a question comes to mind, please, interrupt me, ask your question, this is what we are here for, mainly to interact, to discuss and to break the usual lecture format as much as possible.

Today I would like to present a state, not really of my work, but of hypotheses of my work. I am currently focusing on a history of sexuality which I had the presumption to claim would be in six volumes. I certainly hope not to reach the end, but I do think that there are still a number of questions surrounding this problem of the history of sexuality that could be important if looked at in the right way. I'm not sure I will deal with them appropriately, but maybe asking them is worthwhile nonetheless.

Why undertake a history of sexuality? For me, it would mean the following: something struck me, which is that Freud, psychoanalysis, took as their starting point, their historical starting point, a phenomenon which, at the end of the 19th century, was very important for psychiatry, and even more generally for society, we can even say, for Western culture. This singular phenomenon—that was almost marginal—fascinated doctors, fascinated researchers more generally, one could say; those who were interested in one way or another in the many concerns of psychology. This phenomenon was hysteria. Let's leave aside the purely medical problem of hysteria; hysteria, primarily characterized by a phenomenon of forgetfulness, by a massive misconception of self on the part of the subject, could, with an increase in its hysterical syndrome, become unaware of a whole part of its past or a whole part of its body. Freud showed that that was the anchoring point of psychoanalysis, that it was in fact a misconception by the subject, not of itself generally, but of its desire, or of its sexuality, to use a word that is maybe not a very good one. The subject's misconception of its desire, therefore, from the start. That is the starting point of psychoanalysis, and from there on, this misconception of the subject of its own desire was identified and used by Freud as a general tool for a theoretical analysis and a practical investigation of these illnesses.

What about this misconception of one's own desires? That is the question that Freud ceaselessly posed. Yet, despite the fecundity of this problem, and the richness of the results it lead to, it seems to me that there exists nonetheless another phenomenon, which is almost its opposite, a phenomenon that struck me and that could be called—and here I ask French professors to please cover their ears, as they would banish me from their cenacle, they would ask me never to set foot here, as I will use a word that does not exist—a phenomenon of overknowledge, I mean a knowledge that is in some sense excessive, that is multiplied, a knowledge at once intensive and excessive regarding sexuality, not at the individual level, but at the cultural one, the social one, in theoretical or simplified forms. It seemed to me that Western culture was impacted by a kind of development, of hyper-development of the discourse on sexuality, of the theory of sexuality, the science of sexuality, the knowledge of sexuality.

Perhaps we can say that in Western societies, at the end of the 19th century, there was a very important dual phenomenon: on one hand, a general phenomenon that was discernible only at the individual level, which was the misconception of the subject of his own desire—and it would manifest itself especially in hysteria—and concurrently, on the other hand, a phenomenon of cultural, social, theoretical over-knowledge of sexuality. These two phenomena—the misconception of sexuality by the subject and the over-knowledge of sexuality in society—are not contradictory, they indeed coexist in the West, and one of the problems is to understand how, in a society such as ours, there can be, on the one hand, this theoretical production, this speculative and analytical production surrounding sexuality on the cultural level, and, at the same time, this misunderstanding by the subject of its own sexuality.

As you know, psychoanalysis did not answer this question directly. I don't think we can legitimately say that it didn't touch upon it, but it didn't ignore it altogether either. The tendency of psychoanalysis was to say that in the end, this production, this theoretical, discursive overproduction regarding sexuality in Western societies had in fact only been the product, the result, of a misconception of sexuality that occurs at the individual level and in the subject itself. Better yet, I think that psychoanalysis would say: it is so that subjects remain ignorant about their sexuality and their desire that there exists this whole social production of discourses on sexuality that were also erroneous discourses, irrational discourses, emotional and mythological discourses. Let us say that psychoanalysis only ever approached the knowledge of sexuality in one of two ways: either by taking as a starting point, as an example, as a sort of matrix of the knowledge of sexuality, the famous theories that children entertain about their birth, about whether they have a male organ or not, about the difference between a boy and a girl. Freud tried to think about the knowledge of sexuality from this phantasmatic production found in children, or else to approach it through the great myths of Western religion, but I think psychoanalysts never took very seriously the problem of the production of theories about sexuality in Western societies.

Yet this massive production which dates very far back, at least since Saint Augustin and the first Christian centuries, must be taken seriously and we can't simply reduce it to the models offered by a mythology or a myth, or even a phantasmatic theory. So that my project of doing the history of sexuality inverts this perspective—not to say that psychoanalysis is wrong, not to deny that there exists, in our societies, a miscomprehension on the part of the subject of its own desire, but to say, on one hand, that we should try to study this overproduction of sociocultural knowledge about sexuality for its own sake, in its origins and its forms, and on the other, to try to see to what extent psychoanalysis itself, that in fact thinks of itself as the rational foundation of a knowledge surrounding desire, likely participates in this great economy of the overproduction of the critical knowledge with respect to sexuality. That is what is at stake in the work I want to do; it is not at all a work of anti-psychoanalysis, but aims to rethink the problem of sexuality or rather the knowledge about sexuality, starting not from the miscomprehension of the subject of its own desire, but from the overproduction of social and cultural knowledge, the collective knowledge of sexuality.

If we want to study this overproduction of the theoretical knowledge of sexuality, it seems that the first thing we encounter, the first feature that strikes us in these discourses that Western culture has held about sexuality, is that this discourse very quickly assumed a form we can call scientific. By this I don't mean to say that this discourse has always been rational, I don't mean to say that it has always followed the criteria of what we now call a scientific truth. Long before psychoanalysis, in 19th-century psychiatry, but also in what we can call 18th-century psychology, and, better still, in the moral theology of the 17th century and even the Middle Ages, we can find a whole speculation on what sexuality was, what desire was, and what was, at that particular moment, concupiscence, a whole discourse that claimed to be rational and scientific, and this is where, it seems to me, that we can discern a crucial difference between Western societies and at least a certain number of Eastern ones.

I am referring here to an analysis that I sketched out in an initial volume of *History of Sexuality* that Mr. Watanabe has kindly translated and commented upon, I think, in a journal. It is the opposition between societies that try to maintain a scientific discourse on sexuality as we do in the West, and societies in which the discourse on sexuality is also a very encompassing discourse, a proliferating discourse, a discourse that was multiplied many times over, but doesn't seek to found a science, that seeks, on the contrary, to define an art—an art that would be the art of producing, through sexual intercourse or with sexual organs, a type of pleasure that is sought to be made as intense or as strong as possible or as long-lasting as possible. In many Eastern societies, and also in Ancient Greece and Rome, we can find a whole series of discourses on this possibility, on the search in any case of methods through which to intensify sexual pleasure. The discourse that we find in the West, at least since the Middle Ages, is altogether different from that.

In the West, we do not have erotic art. In other words, we don't learn to make love, we don't learn to give ourselves pleasure, we don't learn to produce pleasure in others, we don't learn to maximize, to intensify, our own pleasure through the pleasure of others. All of this is not taught in the West, and you have neither a discourse nor an initiation other than a clandestine and interindividual to this erotic art. On the other hand, we do have, or we try to have, a sexual science—*scientia sexualis*—on the sexuality of people but not on their pleasure, something that won't be what to do to make pleasure as intense as possible, but what is the truth of this thing that, in the individual, is his sex or his sexuality: the truth about sex and not the intensity of pleasure. I think we have two kinds of analysis, two kinds of research, two kinds of discourses that are entirely different from each other and that we find in two kinds of societies, also very different from each other. I will once again open a small parenthesis: this is obviously something I would very much like to discuss with people whose cultural and historical background is different from mine, and I would like in particular, because there is very little about it in the West, to understand what, in societies such as yours, in Chinese society, erotic art involves, how it developed, on the basis of what knowledge. I think it would be quite interesting in any case to undertake a comparative study of erotic art in Eastern societies and the birth of sexual science in the West ...

Let's return, if we may, to the West itself. What I would like to do in this work on the history of sexuality is precisely the history of this sexual science, this *scientia sexualis*, not in order to say exactly what its different concepts have been, its different theories or its different claims—that could be an entire encyclopedia. But what I am curious about is why Western societies, European societies let's say, have had such a great need for a sexual science, or, in any case, why, for so many centuries and until now, have we tried to constitute a science of sexuality; in other words, why, for thousands of years, have we Europeans wanted to know the truth about sex rather than to reach the intensity of pleasure? To answer this question, it is obvious that we encounter a schema, a very common one, that is the hypothesis that comes immediately to mind and consists in saying the following: here, in the West, of course now thanks to Freud—since Freud—and also after a whole series of different political, social, and cultural movements, we are starting little by little to free sexuality from its constraints, we are starting to allow it to speak, while for so many centuries it had been vowed to silence. We are at once liberating sexuality itself and revealing a condition needed to acknowledge it, while in the preceding centuries, the weight, on the one hand, of bourgeois morality, and on the other, of Christian morality, the first taking over from and in continuity with the second, have prevented us, has prevented the West from really questioning sexuality. In other words, the historical schema that is frequently referred to develops in three stages, three periods.

First: Greek and Roman Antiquity, during which sexuality was free, expressed itself without difficulty, and, indeed, developed, or at least gave itself a discourse in the form of an erotic art. Christianity would then have intervened, the Christianity that for the first time in the history of the West, would strongly prohibit sexuality, saying no to pleasure and even to sex. This no, this interdiction would then have led to a silence on sexuality—a silence based essentially on moral interdictions.

But the bourgeoisie, starting from the 16th century, finding itself in a situation of economic domination and cultural hegemony, would have taken up as its own this Christian asceticism, this Christian refusal of sexuality, and applied it even more strictly and with more rigorous means, thereby prolonging it until the 19th century, when finally, in the very last few years, the veil started to be lifted thanks to Freud.

That is the historical schema that is generally used for the history of sexuality in the West, which is to say that we first focus on the mechanics of repression, of interdiction, of what rejects, excludes, refuses, after which we make Christianity bear the responsibility of this great Western refusal of sexuality. It would be Christianity, then, that said no to sexuality.

I think that this historical schema that has been widely accepted is not accurate and cannot be maintained for a number of reasons. In the book of which Mr. Watanabe has kindly translated a chapter, I mainly questioned problems of method and this emphasis of interdiction and negation which is attributed to the history of sexuality. I tried to show that it would probably be more interesting and productive to do the history of sexuality according to what motivated it and incited it rather than to what forbade it. Anyways, let's leave that for now. I think that we can also object in another way to the traditional schema that I just spoke about, and that is what I would rather talk to you about: an objection not of method but of fact. I am not the one to have formulated this objection of fact; historians have done so—actually one historian of Antiquity whose name is Paul Veyne, and who is currently working on a number of studies on sexuality in the Roman world before Christianity. He has discovered a number of important things that we have to keep in mind.

As you know, in general, when we want to characterize Christian morality with respect to sexuality, and when we want to contrast it with Pagan morality, or with Greek or Roman morality, we use the following arguments: first, it is Christianity that has imposed on ancient societies the rule of monogamy; second, it is Christianity that made of reproduction the function of sexuality, not only as a privileged or principal function, but as its exclusive and only function, that of making love in order to have children. And finally, third, I could have in fact started there, a generalized disqualification of sexual pleasure. Sexual pleasure is a sin—a sin that must be avoided and consequently that must be accorded as small a role as possible. Give sexual pleasure as small a role as possible and only use this pleasure in some sense in spite of itself to have children, and have these children and therefore engage in sexual relations and find pleasure in them only within the confines of marriage, of legitimate and monogamic marriage. These three characteristics are said to define Christianity. Yet the work of Paul Veyne shows that these three main principles of sexual morality existed in the Roman world before the advent of Christianity, and that it is a whole moral system, largely derived from Stoicism, supported by social and ideological structures of the Roman Empire that had started, well before Christianity, to inculcate these principles into the inhabitants of the Roman world, which is to say the sole inhabitants of the world from a European perspective: at that time, marrying and keeping your wife, making love to her to have children, freeing yourself as much as possible from the tyranny of sexual desire, was already something that had been learned by the citizens, the inhabitants of the Roman empire prior to the advent of Christianity. Christianity is therefore not responsible, as it is often said, for this whole set of interdictions, disqualifications, delimitations of sexuality. Polygamy, pleasure outside of marriage, the valorization of pleasure, the indifference towards children had already essentially disappeared from the Roman world before Christianity, and there remained only a small elite, a very small social caste of privileged rich people, rich therefore debauched, that did not practice these principles, but for the most part, they had already been internalized.

Are we to say then that Christianity did not play any role in the history of sexuality? I in fact think that Christianity did play a role, but its role hadn't been so much the introduction of new moral ideas. It hadn't been the introduction, the contribution, the injunction of new interdictions. It seems that what Christianity brought to this history of sexual morality was new techniques. New techniques to impose this morality, or, in effect, a set of new mechanisms of power to inculcate these new moral imperatives or rather these moral imperatives that had already ceased to be new when Christianity penetrated the Roman Empire and became, very quickly, the religion of the State. It is, then, much more in terms of these mechanisms of power than in terms of moral ideas and ethical interdictions that we ought to do the history of sexuality in the Western world since Christianity.

A question, then: what are, then, those new mechanisms of power that Christianity introduced into the Roman world, valorizing those interdictions which were already known and accepted?

This power is what I would call, or rather what is called, the pastorate, which is to say the existence within society of a category of very specific and singular individuals who are defined neither exactly by their status nor exactly by their profession or their individual moral or intellectual qualification, but individuals who, in Christian society, play the role of pastor, of shepherd, with respect to other individuals who are like their sheep or their herd. The introduction of this type of power, this type of dependence, this type of domination within Roman or Ancient society is, I believe, a very important phenomenon.

The first thing we have to note on this subject is that never in Greek or Roman Antiquity had it occurred to anyone that certain individuals could play the role of shepherd in relation to others, guiding them throughout their life, from birth until death. In Greek or Roman literature political figures had never been defined as pastors, or as shepherds. When Plato wonders, in The Statesman, what is a king, what is a patrician, what is the ruler of a city, he does not speak of a shepherd, but of a weaver who brings together the members of a society like threads that he ties together into a beautiful fabric. The idea of a herd does not exist, nor does the idea of a shepherd.

On the other hand, we do find the idea that the leader is, with respect to those over whom he rules, like a shepherd over his herd, not in the Roman world, but in the world of the Eastern Mediterranean. We find it in Egypt, also in Mesopotamia and in Assyria. We find it especially in Hebraic societies where the theme of herd and the shepherd is an absolutely fundamental one, a religious theme, a moral one, and a social one. God is the shepherd of his people. The people of Jehovah are in fact a herd. David, the first king of Israel, receives from the hands of God the task of becoming the shepherd of a people that would become his herd, and the salvation of the Jewish people would be granted, would be secured the day the herd finally returns home and is brought back to the bosom of God. Great importance, therefore, of this pastoral theme in a large number of Eastern Mediterranean societies, while it exists neither for the Greeks nor for the Romans.

This pastoral power that we find in such a developed form in Egypt, Assyria, and for the Hebraic people—in what does it consist and how does it define itself? We can characterize it rapidly by saying that pastoral power contrasts with usual, traditional political power, in that it is not essentially focused on a territory, it rules over a multiplicity of individuals. It rules over sheep, over cattle, over animals. It rules over a herd and a herd in movement. Ruling over a moving multiplicity, that is what characterizes the pastor. It is this power that will be the characteristic pastoral power. Its main function is not so much to ensure victory, as it does not lay claim to a territory. Its primary aim is not conquest, or even the amount of riches or slaves that can be brought back from war. In other words, the main object of pastoral power is not to hurt its enemies, but rather to do good for those under its care. Do good in the most material sense of the term: by nourishing them, giving them subsistence, pasture, leading them to springs, allowing them to drink, finding good prairies. Pastoral power is therefore a power that simultaneously ensures the livelihood of individuals and the livelihood of the group, in contrast with traditional power which manifests itself mainly through the triumph over those subjected to it. It is not a triumphant power; it is a benevolent power.

The third characteristic of this pastoral power is found in the civilizations of which I spoke: as its principal objective is to ensure the livelihood of the herd, it is basically a responsibility, it has as its moral characteristic to be utterly devoted, to sacrifice itself if needed for its sheep. That is what we find in a number of famous biblical texts that are often quoted by commentators: the good pastor, the good shepherd, is he who accepts to sacrifice his life for his sheep. In traditional power, this mechanism is inverted: what makes for a good citizen is the ability to sacrifice himself at the command of the magistrate or to be willing to die for his king. Here, it's the opposite: it's the king, the pastor who accepts to die in order to sacrifice himself.

Finally, and this may be the most important feature, pastoral power is an individualistic one, which is to say that the essential function of a king or magistrate is to save the entirety of the State, the territory, the city, the citizens *en masse*, whereas the good shepherd, the good pastor is able to look after each individual in particular, taken one by one. It isn't an overall power. Of course, the shepherd has to ensure the salvation of the herd, but he has to also ensure the salvation of all of the individuals. We readily find this theme of the shepherd in Hebrew texts and in a certain number of Assyrian or Egyptian ones. A power therefore that pertains to a multiplicity—a multiplicity of individuals in motion, moving from one point to another—an abnegating, sacrificial, individualistic power.

It seems to me that Christianity, from the moment it became, within the Roman Empire, an organizing force both political and social, allowed this type of power to enter into a world that until then had been completely ignorant of it. I'll skip over the way things happened concretely, how Christianity developed like a Church, how, within a Church, priests took on a particular position and status and how they were then obliged to take on a number of responsibilities, how they effectively became the pastors of the Christian community. I think that through the organization of the pastorate in Christian society, starting from the 4th, and even the 3rd century after Christ, a mechanism of power developed that would be very important for the history of Christianity in the West and, in a specific manner, for sexuality as well.

In a general sense, what does it mean for Western men to live in a society where this type of pastoral power exists?

First: having a pastor implies that for each individual, it is necessary to seek salvation. In other words, for the Christian West, salvation is at once an individual question—we each have to seek our salvation—but it is not a question of choice. Christian societies did not allow individuals the freedom to say: "Actually, I don't want to be saved". Every individual was required to seek their salvation: "You will be saved, or rather, you will do everything it takes to be saved, and we will start punishing you already in this world if you don't do everything needed to be saved". The power of the pastor lies precisely in his authority to oblige people to do everything it takes for their salvation: an obligatory salvation.

Second: this obligatory salvation is not done alone. We do it for ourselves, of course, but we can only do it if we accept the authority of another. By accepting the authority of another, every one of our actions will have to be known, or in any case could be known, by the pastor who has the authority over the individual or many individuals, who, consequently, can say yes or no: that is how things should be done, we know that they cannot be done otherwise. This means that to the old judicial structures that all societies had long been acquainted with—that there are a number of accepted laws whose infractions are punished—another type of behavioral analysis is added on, another form of culpabilization, of condemnation, one that is much finer, much tighter, much more upheld: the one that is ensured by the pastor. The pastor can force people to do whatever is necessary for their salvation and he is in a position to supervise, and certainly to maintain over others a continuous surveillance and control.

Third: in a Christian society, the pastor is someone who can ask for absolute obedience from others, which is a very important and new phenomenon. Gallo-Roman societies, of course, had known laws and magistrates, and an imperial power that was an entirely autocratic one. But never would one have had, in Greek and Roman Antiquity, the idea of asking of someone for total, absolute, and unconditional obedience to someone else. Yet this is precisely what happened with the emergence of the pastor and the pastorate in Christian society. The pastor can impose his will on others, and according to his own decision, without there even being general rules or laws, because, and that is what is important in Christianity: people don't obey in order to arrive at a certain result, they don't obey, for instance, simply to acquire a habit, an aptitude or even a merit. In Christianity, the utmost merit is precisely to be obedient. Obedience must lead to a state of obedience. Remaining obedient is the requisite condition for all other virtues. Obedient with respect to whom? Obedient to the pastor. It is a system of generalized obedience, and the famous Christianity humility is nothing other than a sort of interiorized form of this obedience. I am humble, which means that I will accept orders from whoever gives them to me, and I am able to recognize in this will of the other—mine being last—the very will of God.

Finally, and this is something that I believe will bring us back to our initial problem, which is the history of sexuality, the pastorate brought with it a whole series of techniques and procedures that deal with truth and the production of truth. The Christian pastor teaches, and in doing so he follows, of course, the tradition of the masters of wisdom or masters of truth such as the ancient philosophers and pedagogues. He teaches truth, he teaches writing, he teaches morality, he teaches God's commandments and the commandments of the Church. In this way he is then a master, but the Christian pastor is also a master of truth in another sense. In order to fulfill his duty, the Christian pastor has to know everything his sheep are doing, everything the herd is doing, what every member of the herd is doing at every moment, but he also has to know from the inside everything that is happening in the soul, the heart, the deepest secrets of each individual. This knowledge of the interiority of individuals is absolutely required for the practice of the Christian pastorate.

What does it mean to know the interiority of individuals? It means that the pastor will have at his disposal ways of analyzing, reflecting on, and detecting what goes on, but also that the Christian will be obliged to tell his pastor everything that is going on in the depth of his soul; in particular, he will have to resort to this practice that I believe is so specific to Christianity: a constant and exhaustive confession. The Christian must continually confess to someone who will be in charge of guiding his conscience, and this exhaustive confession will produce a truth that was obviously not known to the pastor, but also not to the subject either; it is this truth, obtained through the examination of conscience, through confession, this production of truth that develops alongside the direction of conscience, the direction of souls, that will constitute the sort of permanent link between the shepherd and his herd and to each member of his herd. The truth, the production of an interior truth, the production of subjective truth, is a fundamental element of the practice of the pastor.

We have now arrived at the very problem of sexuality. What did Christianity have to deal with as it was developing, starting from the 2nd and the 3rd century? It had to deal with a Roman society that had already accepted, for the most part, its morality, the morality of monogamy, of sexuality, of reproduction that I was telling you about. Also, Christianity had before it, or rather next to it, or behind it, a model of intense religious life that was Hindu, Buddhist monasticism, and the Christian monks that had spread throughout the Eastern Mediterranean starting in the 3rd century had adopted, to a large extent, ascetic practices. Christianity always found itself caught between a civil society that had accepted a certain number of moral imperatives and this ideal of absolute asceticism; it tried, on one hand, to master this model of Buddhist asceticism, to interiorize it all while controlling it, and, on the other, to usurp it in order to be able to lead this civil society of the Roman empire from the inside.

Through what means would it be able to do so? I think it is the very difficult and also very opaque conception of the flesh that enabled, that allowed for the establishment of this sort of balance between an asceticism that turned away from the world and a civil society that was a secular one. I think that Christianity found a way of establishing a type of power that controlled individuals through their sexuality, conceived as something to be wary of, something that always introduced into individuals the possibility of temptation and of a downfall. But at the same time, it was absolutely not—for then one would fall into radical asceticism—about the refusal of everything that could come from the body as being harmful, as being evil. The body had to be allowed its pleasures, its sexuality, to function within a society that had its needs, its requirements, that had its organization of the family and its need for reproduction. A conception that was then, in fact, relatively moderate with regard to sexuality such that Christian flesh was never conceived of as an absolute evil that had to be eliminated, but rather as the perpetual source within subjectivity, within individuals, of a temptation that could potentially lead the individual beyond the boundaries imposed by common morality, which is to say marriage, monogamy, the sexuality of reproduction, and the limitation and disqualification of pleasure.

It was therefore a moderate morality between asceticism and civil society that Christianity established and operated through this apparatus of the pastorate, but whose main components rested upon this knowledge that was both external and internal, a meticulous and detailed knowledge of individuals by themselves and by others. In other words, it is through the constitution of a subjectivity, an awareness of self that is constantly attuned to one's own weaknesses, one's own temptations, one's own flesh; it is through the constitution of this subjectivity that Christianity managed to make this rather ordinary, relatively uninteresting morality function between asceticism and the civil society. This internalizing technique, this technique of self-awareness regarding one's weaknesses, one's body, one's sexuality, one's flesh, was, it seems to me, Christianity's main contribution to the history of sexuality. The flesh is the very subjectivity of the body; Christian flesh is sexuality taken from within this subjectivity, this subjugation of the individual to himself which is the primary effect of the introduction of pastoral power into Roman society. It seems to me that it's in this way that we can understand—all of this is a series of hypotheses, of course—the real role Christianity played in the history of sexuality. Not, therefore, interdiction and refusal, but the putting in place of a mechanism of power and control that was at the same time a mechanism of knowledge, of knowledge about individuals, but also a knowledge of individuals about themselves and with respect to themselves. All of this constitutes the specific imprint of Christianity, and that is why I think one can do the history of sexuality in Western societies starting from mechanisms of power.

This is then, very schematically laid out, the framework of what I've undertaken. It's simply a framework, nothing is certain, they are just hypotheses that you can just throw back at me as queries. Of course, if you have any objections, suggestions, criticisms, confirmations, I would be delighted to hear them.

DEBATE

S. Hasumi: Asking questions of Mr. Foucault is not an easy task, but not so much because of my ignorance or timidity. The difficulty comes precisely from the clarity of his presentation. We are all used to this clarity thanks to his writings. In all of his books, he announces each time in a precise manner the problem he will be dealing with and through what means he will analyze it, as he tries to define the conditions and the circumstances that make his work necessary, and what we have just heard confirms this clarity and this precision. Here, once again, he was careful to answer all the questions in advance and preemptively respond to any objections that could arise. I therefore have almost nothing to ask him, but in order to get the discussion going, I would like to simply ask him the following.

In your inaugural class at the Collège de France, I seem to remember you treating sexuality through the angle of repression and exclusion: the discourse on sexuality was subject to interdictions and rarified. But, starting with *The Will to Knowledge*, you no longer treat sexuality as the object of repression, but rather as something that proliferates in a scientific field. In this regard, people often speak of a change in Michel Foucault, and some have been quite happy about this change …

M. Foucault: …. and others who aren't happy at all.

S. Hasumi: I personally don't think this is the case. You haven't changed, you haven't abandoned the repression hypothesis, but you have questioned it in order to formulate the problem of power in a different way …

M. Foucault: I thank you for this question, which in fact is important and was worth asking. You formulated it, I think, in the best possible way.

It is true that even in recent texts, I have mainly referred to a concept of power and mechanisms of power that was, in some sense, juridical. The analyses I am trying to do, and I'm by no means the only one trying to do so, are clearly partial and fragmented. It isn't at all about constructing a theory of power, a general theory of power, nor to say

what power is and where it comes from. For centuries, and even mil-
lennia in the West, we have posed this question, and it isn't certain
that the answers have been satisfactory. What I am trying to do is, at
an empirical level, to take things from the middle, so to speak. Not:
"Where does power come from, where does it go?" but: "How does
it circulate and how does it work, what are all the relations of power,
how can we describe some of the main relations of power that are at
work in our society?"

I therefore don't conceive of power in the sense of a government,
or of a State. What I say is: between different people, in a family, in a
university, in a barrack, in a hospital, in a medical consultation there
are power relations at play. What are they, what do they lead to, how
do they tie individuals to one another, why are they tolerated, why, in
other cases, are they not? Let us conduct this analysis, if you will, from
the middle and empirically. That is the first thing.

As for the second, I am not the first, far from it, to have tried.
Psychoanalysts, Freud, and many of his successors, in particular
Marcuse, Reich, etc. have also questioned not so much the origin of
power or the foundation of power, or its legitimacy, or its global forms,
but how it works in the psyche of an individual, in an individual's
unconscious, or in the economy of desire—how it is play out in relations of power. What does the father, for instance, have to do with the
individual's desire? Or how is the interdiction of masturbation, or even
father–mother relations, the distribution of roles, etc. inscribed in the
psyche of children. So they too, of course, were analyzing mechanisms
of power, relations of power, from the middle and empirically.

But what struck me was that these analyses always considered that
power had as its function and role to say no, to forbid, to prevent,
to mark a limit, and consequently, power had as its main effect all
the phenomena of exclusion, hysterization, obliteration, of hiding, of
forgetting or, if you will, of the constitution of the unconscious. The
unconscious certainly constitutes itself—psychoanalysts will say I am
being hasty—on the basis of a relation of power. This conception or
idea that mechanisms of power are always forbidding mechanisms was,
I think, widespread. It was an idea that had, one could say, a political

advantage, an immediate advantage, and was therefore almost dangerous because it allows one to say: "Let's get rid of the interdictions and then that's it, the power will have disappeared, we will be free the day we get rid of the restrictions". But that is maybe too hasty ...

In any case, I've changed quite a bit in that regard. I changed after I did a detailed study, as precise as possible, on prisons and systems of surveillance and punishment in Western societies in the 18th and 19th centuries, especially the end of the 18th. It seemed to me that in Western societies we witnessed the development, at the same time as capitalism in fact, of a whole series of procedures, a whole series of techniques to take charge of, to watch over, to control the behavior of individuals, their gestures, their ways of doing things, where they lived, their aptitudes, but the main function of these mechanisms was not to forbid.

Of course they forbade and punished, but the main objective of these types of power—and what made them effective and strong— was to allow, to force individuals to multiply their efficacy, their forces, their aptitudes, in short, everything that made it possible for them to be used in society's production apparatus: train them, place them where they are most useful, form them so they have one capacity or other; that is what the army tried to do, starting in the 17th century, when the great disciplines were imposed, something had had been unknown earlier. Western armies didn't used to be disciplined, they became disciplined, soldiers were called to exercise, to walk in rows, to shoot with rifles, to handle rifles in a certain way in order to maximize the army's usefulness. In the same way, there had been a whole training of the working class, or rather of what was not yet the working class, but of workers capable of working in big workshops, or even in small family or artisanal ones, who had been taught to get used to living in a certain place, to manage their families. A production of individuals therefore, a production of individuals' abilities, of individuals' productivity; all that was obtained through power mechanisms in which interdictions existed, but they existed simply as instruments. For the most part, this disciplinarization of individuals was not negative.

You can say and believe that this was catastrophic, you can add all the negative moral and political adjectives you want, but what I mean to say is that the mechanism wasn't essentially an interdiction, but a production, an intensification, a multiplication. At that point I said to myself: in the societies in which we live, does power really have, as a form and as a goal, to forbid and to say no? Aren't power mechanisms more deeply inscribed in our societies than that, aren't they what is able to produce something, aren't they what is able to multiply, to intensify? And this is this hypothesis that I'm now trying to apply to sexuality: sexuality, it would seem, is in fact the most forbidden thing we can imagine; we are endlessly forbidding children to masturbate, teenagers to make love before marriage, adults to make love in in a certain way with a certain person. The world of sexuality is a world filled with interdictions.

But it seemed to me that in Western societies, these interdictions were accompanied by a whole discursive production that is very intense and large—scientific discourses, institutional discourses—and at the same time by a worry, a real obsession about sexuality that can already be seen very clearly in the Christian morality of the 16th and the 17th century, during the Reformation and Counter-Reformation—an obsession that so far hasn't ended.

Western man—I don't know if this is the case in your society—has always considered that the most important thing in his life was his sexuality. And increasingly so. In the 16th century, the ultimate sin was the sin of the flesh. So if sexuality was simply eliminated, forbidden, forgotten, rejected, denied, why is it that there is such a proliferation of discourse, such a dread of sexuality? The hypothesis from which my analyses proceed—that I may not follow through completely because it may not be the right one—would be that the West does not in fact negate sexuality—it doesn't exclude it—but it introduced it and shaped on the basis of it a whole complex apparatus that involves the constitution of individuality, of subjectivity, in short, of the ways we behave and become conscious of ourselves. In other words, in the West, people are individualized through a certain number of procedures, and I think that sexuality, rather than being just one element of individuals that could be erased from them, is constitutive of this link that obliges people to tie with their identities in the form of a subjectivity.

Perhaps this is the clarity Mr. Hasumi spoke of, and I would say the cost of wanting to be clear … I dislike opacity because I consider it to be a form of despotism; one has to be open to making mistakes and to stumble a bit and I fear that I have stumbled. And if I did give you that impression, it's certainly because I have!

Translated by Zineb Belghiti

6

THE THEATER OF PHILOSOPHY

"Tetsugaku no butai" ("La scène de la philosophie"); an interview with M. Watanabe, April 2, 1978, in Sekai, July 1978, pp. 312–332.

Theater and French literature specialist, Moriaki Watanabe, who introduced M. Foucault to traditional forms of Japanese theater, was in the process of translating The Will to Knowledge.

Dits et écrits III, no.234

M. Watanabe: The themes of the theater and the gaze recur so insistently in your writing that they seem to govern the very structure of your discourse. Why is that?

M. Foucault: I think this is a very important question. Western philosophy has paid little attention to the theater, perhaps ever since Plato condemned it. We have to wait until Nietzsche for the question of the relationship between theater and philosophy to be raised again with acuity in Western philosophy. In fact, I think Western philosophy's

DOI: 10.4324/9781003303763-8

discrediting of the theater is related to a way of approaching the question of the gaze. Since Plato and even more so since Descartes, one of the most interesting philosophical questions is about what it means to look at something, or rather what it means to know if what we're looking at is true or illusory, whether our world is real or deceptive. The very purpose of philosophy is to separate reality from illusion, truth from deception. Theater, however, ignores these distinctions entirely. There's no point in asking if theater is true, if it's illusory, if it's deceptive; the very act of raising the question makes theater disappear. Accepting the non-difference between truth and falsehood, between reality and illusion, is the very condition of the existence of theater. Without being a theater specialist of your caliber, and without having considered the problem of theater as deeply as you have, there's something that interests and fascinates me. What I'd like to do is to try and describe how Westerners viewed things without ever questioning whether they were true. I'd like to try and describe how, through the play of their gazes, they staged a view of the world. It in fact doesn't matter to me whether psychiatry is true or false, and in any case, this isn't the question I'm asking. It doesn't matter to me whether medicine says falsehoods or truths. It matters to those who are ill, but to me as an analyst, if you will, it's not what interests me, especially since I'm not qualified to separate truth from falsehood. But I'd like to know how we staged illness, how we staged madness, how we staged crime, for example, in other words, how we perceived and internalized it, and assigned value to illness, crime, and madness. I'd like to know what role we made them play; I'd like to tell the story of the *stage* on which we then tried to distinguish what is true from what is false. But this distinction is not what interests me; what does is the constitution of the stage and of the theater. The theater of truth is what I'd like to describe. How the West built a theater of truth, a stage of truth, a stage for rationality which has now become a mark of Western imperialism now that the economy of the West has perhaps reached its peak. The essence of the Western ways of life and means of political domination have likely reached their end. But there is something that remains, something the West left to the rest of the world, and that's a kind of rationality. It's a certain kind of perception of truth and of error, a certain theater of truth and falsehood.

M. Watanabe: The pleasure I get from reading your work and its overlap with theater—what Barthes calls the "pleasure of the text"—is certainly due to your way of writing: the dramatic structure of your discourse, whether it's in *Discipline and Punish* or in *The Will to Knowledge*. The pleasure of reading certain chapters of *The Order of Things* is equal to that of reading great political tragedies by Racine, *Britannicus*, for example.

M. Foucault: I'm flattered, too flattered.

M. Watanabe: While you may disagree, I don't think it's wrong to consider you as the last great classical writer. It's not because, dare I say, I know Racine's work well that I'm sensitive to the stylistic elements of your books. It's simply because your description of the forces that shaped the great epistemological or institutional mutations of the West aligns with a certain style and conception of writing. For example, in a special edition of the journal *Arc*, "La crise dans la tête"—an edition dedicated to Michel Foucault, which you declined, saying that a special edition is usually a kind of burial—there's an interview you did with Fontana which was first published in Italy. In it, you address the necessity of "differentiating between events, between the platforms and levels they belong to, and of rebuilding the threads that link them together and cause one to entail another". You insisted on "rejecting analyses which refer to the symbolic field or to the domain of significant structures", instead of resorting to "analyses done in terms of the genealogy of relations of power, of strategic developments, of tactics". We shouldn't refer to "a great model of languages and signs" but to "the war and battle", because "the historicity that carries and determines us is a historicity of belligerence", not "a historicity of language". We shouldn't look for a "relation of meaning" but a "relation of power". However, as Barthes has observed, Racine's tragedy is dictated by power relations, which themselves depend on a dual relation of passion and power. The strategy of passion for Racine is absolutely belligerent. There's a kind of realism in theatrical and belligerent confrontations that surely explains the genealogical overlap I see between your writing and Racine's.

Theater as a dramatical representation was, at least in Western culture, the perfect example of a confrontation on the stage, in other words on the "battlefield", the ultimate space of strategies and tactics. If the gaze in your writing is reminiscent of the great genius of classical French dramaturgy, it's because it knows how to ignite these great historical confrontations which were, up until now, either forgotten or unknown.

M. Foucault: You're absolutely right. The reason I'm not a philosopher in the traditional sense—and maybe I'm no philosopher at all; in any case, I'm not a good one—is that I'm not interested in the eternal, in what doesn't move or what remains stable beneath the glimmer of appearance. I'm interested in the event, which was never a branch of philosophy, except perhaps for the Stoics for whom it was a problem of logic. But even then, I believe Nietzsche was the first to define philosophy as an activity which allows us to know what is happening and what is happening now. In other words, there are processes, motions, forces unknown to us but that move us, and it's up to the philosopher to diagnose them, to diagnose the present.

The question is: who are we? What is happening? These two questions differ greatly from the traditional ones: what is the soul? What is eternity? A philosophy of the present, of the event, of what is happening, tries by way of philosophy to understand what theater deals with. For theater always deals with an event, the paradox of the theater being that this event repeats itself, repeats itself every night, because we enact it, and repeats itself indefinitely or at least for an indefinite amount of time, because it is always a reference to a prior event that is repeatable.

Theater captures the event and stages it.

It's true that in my books I try to capture an event that seemed, or still seems to me, to be important in our present. For example, at one point in time, the West differentiated between madness and non-madness; at another, there was a certain way of understanding the intensity of crime and the human problem raised by crime. It seems to me that we repeat all these events. We repeat them in the present, and I'm trying to determine what event has defined our lives and in what way it continues to affect us.

Hence these books that are—you're absolutely right, I really do flatter myself by speaking so indulgently—well, theatrical dramas. I understand what an inconvenience this is; I risk granting too much importance to an event by incorrectly representing it as something dramatic or major. Hence my flaw—we must speak of our flaws along with our projects—that is, maybe a kind of intensification or dramatization of events that ought to be spoken of with less passion. But ultimately, we have to give a chance to those secret events that shimmer in the past and still impact our present.

M. Watanabe: What you say about secret events strikes me as very important, especially since the inflation or over-valorization of events in the media could risk disqualifying the event as an event. Events are representations spread by mass media and there's a kind of skepticism about them. You, however, try to reclaim the event as a real mutational factor. The themes of the gaze, of the stage, of dramaturgy, of the event are all logically connected to the notion of space. Already in the preface of *The Birth of the Clinic*, you stated that the book "is about space, language, and death" before promptly adding that it is "about the gaze". If you'll allow for such a schematization, it seems to me that the paradigm of your analysis and discourse is made up of a certain number of terms or patterns such as "space", "language", "death", "gaze" and that death is replaced by "madness", "crime", or an episteme depending on what is being analyzed.

Space is the most important of these motifs and is very closely linked to theater. Up until *Discipline and Punish*, your analysis offered to investigate the unique nature of the origin and implementation of a specific enclosed space. Clinics, psychiatric hospitals, and prisons were all enclosed spaces that were established through an isolation from the rest of the social body while, at the same time, remaining topologically inside the city. A typical example is the great confinement of mad people in the 17th century that you analyzed in *History of Madness*.

As you mentioned yesterday during the seminar at the University of Tokyo, your analysis then focuses on the mechanisms of power within the judicial system. Allow me to briefly comment on a different type of isolation, the isolation of speech in Mallarmé's work, as it represents the fundamental poetic experience in Western modernity. You have pointed this out yourself in our interview eight years ago: since Höderlin, modern literature is viewed as mad, and as a result it established itself as *another* language, different from ordinary language, which functions like a currency. And this language, isolated by its very status of social exclusion, ended up resembling another excluded language, the language of madness which you once named "the work of fire" in reference to Blanchot. I bring up this episode simply to say that Foucault's fans in Japan were initially people who read Foucault's writings on Western literary modernity from Mallarmé to Bataille to Klossovski.

As a result, your analysis doesn't focus on the content of these isolated, enclosed, and debarred spaces, but rather on the instruments of power that rely on them, while also acknowledging the limit of their efficacy. In that sense, it's less about the dramaturgy that plays out inside these spaces—which are all the more important as they are enclosed and isolated—as it is about the staging and implementation of the *dispositif* that makes such a dramaturgy of space possible.

The beginning of *Discipline and Punish* is exemplary: the great ceremonial and bloody theatricality of Damien's torture is followed by the cold and meticulous regulations of a correctional facility for young delinquents. The very refusal of theatricality, or at least its invisibility in the disciplinary case files, turns out to be of the same order as the process of internalizing the theatrical aspect of the power apparatus Bentham had envisioned for his Panopticon. Regardless, in your books, the distribution and reorganization of social spaces are perceived as strategic factors of the power apparatus.

M. Foucault: Absolutely. When I was a student, French philosophy was dominated by a kind of latent Bergsonism. I say Bergsonism, but that doesn't mean it was the real Bergson—far from it. It favored analyses of space as opposed to time, which was viewed as something frozen and dead. I believe this is an important anecdote about the renewed Bergsonism we were still living in: I remember giving a lecture at an architecture school and speaking about the different forms of differentiated spaces in a society such as ours. At the end, someone spoke up in a very violent tone and argued that to speak about space was to be an agent of capitalism, that everyone knows that space is dead, frozen, and represents the immobility that the bourgeois society wants to impose on itself, that it's to misunderstand the great movement of history, it's to misunderstand dialectics and revolutionary dynamism ... By this sort of valorization of a Bergsonian approach that favors time over space, you could easily see how he was developing a vulgar, very vulgar, conception of Marxism. Anecdote aside, it is emblematic of the way a certain Hegelian and Marxist conception of history took over from and intensified a Bergsonian valorization of time.

M. Watanabe: This is the episode you mentioned in the introductory debate for the reprinted edition of the French translation of the Panopticon.

M. Foucault: That's it. But I think it's important to understand how space was in fact an integral part of history, which is to say how a society configured its space to establish relations of power. And by the way, there's nothing original in this; for example, agricultural historians have shown how spatial distributions translated, but also reinforced, inscribed, and anchored power relations, economic relations ... It seemed important to me to show how a new form of spatiality within society, a way of socially and politically distributing spaces came about in the industrial capitalist societies which emerged in the 16th century, and that it's possible to do the history of an entire country, culture, or society based on the way space is valorized and distributed. I think the first space to highlight the problem of the social and historical differences between societies is the space of exclusion, of exclusion and confinement.

In Greco-Roman and especially Greek societies, when you wanted to get rid of an individual, you'd exile him. Greek theater illustrates this well. This means that there was always another space. There was always the possibility of moving to a different space whose existence the city was not meant to acknowledge, or at least in which it had no intention of introducing its laws or its values. The Greek world was divided into autonomous cities, all of which were surrounded by a barbaric world. Spaces have thus always been polymorphic and versatile, and there has always been a separation between spaces and emptiness, the outside, and the undefined. There's no doubt that we now live in a crowded world: the earth has become round, overpopulated. Like in Greek society, in the Middle Ages it was common practice to deal with bothersome individuals by exiling them. It's important to remember that during this time, the main form of punishment was banishment: "Get lost and make sure we don't see you around here anymore". And we'd brand those individuals to ensure they wouldn't come back. Same for the mad. By the 17th century, the population had reached a level of relative density—though incomparable to ours today—, but it made us believe that the world was full. And once we addressed the organization of space within the State, or better yet within Europe—Europe as a political and economic entity established itself at the end of the 16th, beginning of the 17th century—, at that time, getting rid of someone was neither possible nor accepted. Hence the need to create exclusionary spaces, but spaces that no longer serve just for banishment or exile but are at the same time inclusionary spaces: to rid yourself by confining. It seems to me that the practice of confinement is one of the consequences of a crowded and enclosed world. To put it briefly, confinement is a consequence of the fertility of the Earth.

At this point, a whole series of spatial mutations took arose; contrary to popular belief, the Middle Ages were a time when people were always moving; borders were nonexistent, people were perfectly mobile; monks, academics, merchants, and sometimes even peasants would move around as soon as they had no more land wherever they were from. Great voyages didn't start in the 16th century, far from it. But in Western society, social space began to stabilize between the 16th and 17th centuries with urban organization, structures of ownership, surveillance, and road networks ... That was when we arrested the nomads, put the poor away, and stopped the beggars, and the world froze. But it was able to freeze only under the condition that we institutionalize different spaces for the sick, the mad, the poor, that we distinguish the rich neighborhoods from the poor ones, unhealthy neighborhoods from comfortable ones ... This differentiation of spaces is a part of our history and is certainly one that we have in common.

M. Watanabe: In Japan, we have a historically similar but also different experience: the Tokugawa shogunate's decision, in the 17th century, to relegate the pleasure district and the theater to a peripheral space outside of the city. This spatial distinction and topological separation was maintained until the Meiji restoration. Social discrimination was expressed materially through urban space. I'd also like to talk about the fascination of certain artists—specifically Western playwrights—with spaces external to the Western world. From Claudel to Artaud to Brecht, and more recently from Grotowsky to the Théâtre du Soleil, it's become clear that since the end of the 19th century, certain playwrights and directors became attracted to some forms of traditional eastern theater, as something closer to the origins of theater that didn't fit within the historical Western mold. The Rousseauist pursuit of origins turned towards spaces outside of Europe, becoming a search for the other, for what lies outside of Western civilization. This movement can't be boiled down to a simple cultural variation of Western powers' imperialism. What is certain is the appeal of a space governed by a different notion of time, different from the theo-teleological time of the West. At the same time, from Durkheim to Mauss, ethnology also established an entirely different space as its investigative field.

The resurgence of the thematic of space from 1950 to1960 was certainly one of the most interesting moments in the history of ideas, where from Maurice Blanchot's The Literary Space (1955) to Jean-Luc Godard's Pierrot le Fou (1965), within the field of literary criticism, the field of experimental creation, of human sciences, the revalorization of space overthrew the all-powerful predominance of unequivocal time and history.

It is certainly superfluous to add that it's precisely during this period that a certain theoretical discourse, which we rightly or wrongly call structuralism, began to take shape. The case of Lévi-Strauss is a perfect example: in order to ensure the search for a structural anthropology, it was absolutely necessary that the scope and method of his investigation be freed from the Hegelian, theo-teleological conception of time. This act of liberation was only possible thanks to this plurality of spaces and their differentiation from Western space.

M. Foucault: Yes, structuralism, what we called structuralism, never really existed beyond a few thinkers, ethnologists, historians of religions and linguists, but what we called structuralism was characterized, precisely, by a liberation from or an overcoming of the long-privileged Hegelian understanding of history.

M. Watanabe: But it's also wrong to conflate the refusal of this Hegelian privilege of history with a renewed valorization of events, of the event as a concept, is that correct?

M. Foucault: Or, on the contrary—I won't speak on behalf of Lévi-Strauss, he can speak for himself, and he's come here to speak about this—it was, at least for me, a way of bringing the event to the surface and of undertaking historical analyses. I'm known as a structuralist and anti-historian when, in reality, I have nothing to do with structuralism and I am in fact a historian. But I treat the events that dictate the organization and structuring of certain cultural spaces as important historical objects, or objects of an analysis which takes place over time. That's my first object of inquiry.

Hence the confusion; you know, critics in France—I'm not sure how it is in Japan—are all somewhat hasty. They easily confuse what one talks about with what has been said. It's enough to talk about space for people to believe that one is a spatio-centrist who hates history and time. This is nonsense.

M. Watanabe: There are pretty direct echoes of this in Japan as well.

M. Foucault: That aside, it's true that in the '50s there was a way to set yourself apart from a certain way of writing about history without negating or refusing it, without criticizing historians, but only in order to write history differently. Look at Barthes, he's a historian in my opinion. But he didn't do history the way we had until then. But this was perceived as a refusal of history.

What was interesting was to see how philosophers interpreted this as refusal of history. Because the historians weren't wrong; they saw the work people were doing, what the so-called structuralists were doing, and they read them as historical works. They accepted them and appreciated them, and then they critiqued them as historical works.

M. Watanabe: We know that you often refer to the historian Fernand Braudel and to his work on the Mediterranean world.

M. Foucault: Precisely, among all the great historians of what we call the *Annales* school in France—I know it wasn't all of them, but the majority—one of its founders, Marc Bloch, was interested in the rural space and had tried to do its history. It's important to see that structuralism, what we call structuralism, tried to make a different kind of time emerge. In other words, there wasn't only one kind of time, in Hegelian or Bergsonian fashion, a kind of big, all-encompassing flow that would carry everything with it. There are different histories which overlap. Braudel did very interesting work on these different durations: certain elements remain stable for a long time while others break away, and finally there are events whose outcomes or lasting effects have different scopes and values; so a brief time and lengthy durations; the difficulty consists in analyzing these interactions within the context of time.

M. Watanabe: I'm not sure if this is just a coincidence or a historical necessity, but this resurgence of the problem of space coincides with the end of French colonialism.

M. Foucault: Yes, I hadn't thought of this point, but I think we can connect the end of the colonial era with this idea. This means, first, that

European space is not the only space, that we live in a series of polymorphous spaces and, second, the idea that there isn't just one history, that there are multiple histories, multiple times, multiple durations, multiple speeds which all intertwine, cross over, and make up events. One event is not a segment of time, it's the point of intersection between two durations, two speeds, two evolutions, two historical trajectories.

M. Watanabe: After all, imperial colonialism was the translation of an obsession with unequivocal time applied to a different space, one which must adapt to the Western mold.

M. Foucault: In some way, the focus of my work is imperial colonialism specifically within European space. How forms of domination over individuals, or over a certain category of individuals, establish themselves and allow Western societies, modern societies, to function.

There is one example, which was never studied closely but fascinates me and served as a guiding force, even though I myself have not analyzed it closely enough. It's the problem of the army, the European army. In fact, before the modern era, Europe had never been made up of military states. Feudalism was not exactly a military system, it was a complex judicial system in which, at various points, certain categories of individuals had to go to war. But they weren't soldiers and, despite this, their main purpose was still to help the efforts of war. Society also wasn't organized as a large army or according to the structure of a permanent army. Something like the Roman legion, which Rome used as a model for colonization and whose structure was modeled after the Romans living along the Danube, in Romania, or on the coast of the Rhine, for example, none of that existed; a feudalist spatial organization wasn't a military one, even if society's main actors, even those that held the power, were also at the same time soldiers. European armies were always something transitory. There would come a time or a season, which always happened to be during the summer, when they went to war. When the war was over and often even before it ended, people would regroup and leave. So people were always both at war and at peace, there were moments of war but there was no military space. Armies would disperse, then reassemble, and then disperse again.

At the beginning of the 17th century, permanent armies started to form, so naturally they had to be placed somewhere. Also, they had specific weapons, cannons, and particularly rifles that necessarily implied that operations, the placement of military units, the arrangements adopted to engage in battle, be the result of a meticulous calculation and speculation. This meant that the army's spatial arrangement was dual in nature: it existed permanently and needed to be dispersed within the country; its movements, deployment, and way of engaging in battle had to obey very specific spatial laws. This is when the army's discipline and knowledge intervened to overthrow the front, to transform the military formation into a front ...

The army became a sort of spatial model; gridded plans for the camps, for example, became models for cities, like the gridded cities that started to appear in Italy during the Renaissance, then in Sweden and in Germany in the 17th century; the temptation to construct a city modeled after the army, a desire expressed by many planners in the 17th and especially 18th century, was very strong; there was a dream of a military society. Both Napoleon and Prussian societies were expressions of this dream. What we see here is a perfect problem of the history of space.

M. Watanabe: A beautiful article by Deleuze about your book *Discipline and Punish* was entitled "A writer, no, a new cartographer".[1] Deleuze insisted on a sort of mutation which had taken place between *Archaeology of Knowledge* and *Discipline and Punish*. Up until *Archaeology of Knowledge*, your analysis focused on statements or spoken words. But with *Discipline and Punish*, you began to focus on their underlying foundation, the surface on which they appeared—on the confines of language, space, ground, surface which they divided up like a diagram. Your analysis began to focus not only on what was said at a certain point in history, but also on the things that were happening at the same time. Your goal was to uncover the immanence of power relations which made these statements possible.

M. Foucault: That's it. Let's say that from my point of view, my primary focus was the history of science. Phenomenology didn't deal with this. You won't find analyses of the constitution of scientific knowledge in

Sartre's work, not even in Merleau-Ponty's. This isn't a criticism, it's just an observation.

I was a student of the historians of sciences, of Canguilhem for example. My goal was to determine whether it would be possible to do a history of science that aims to retrace the birth, development, and organization of a science based not on its rational internal structure but on the external elements that have in fact served as its support.

Because of this I've always, or at least for a while, alternated between the internal analysis of scientific discourses, and the analysis of the external conditions of their existence. In *History of Madness*, I tried to show how psychiatry developed, the themes it addressed, the topics it focused on, and the concepts it used, while at the same time, I tried to grasp the historical ground on which all of this happened, in other words the practices of confinement, the change in the social and economic conditions of the 17th century. In *The Order of Things*, I returned to this problem, but this time I focused only on the problem of scientific discourse itself, without considering the historical context in which it played out; the analysis in *The Order of Things* is, essentially, an analysis of things said and the rules of their formation.

But something else remained unresolved—it was mentioned to me many times, but I was also aware of it: an analysis of the external conditions of existence, operation, and evolution of these scientific discourses. Only I wasn't satisfied with the explanations that were given to me at the time, the ones suggested to me and that I was criticized for not using. I don't believe that we can solve this problem by referring to relations of production or to the ideology of a dominant class. The examples of madness or illness—of psychiatry and of medicine—seem to show that in order to find the point of emergence of the organization and development of a field of knowledge, we have to look at the relations of power within society.

Because I'm slow, it took me a long time to understand all of this. But I came to realize that in order to do the history of the staging of truth, of this theater of truth you're talking about, we have to look at the relations between power and knowledge. What set the stage for truth in the West? I don't think it's the State as an acknowledged entity of power, but rather the relations of power, which are themselves obviously intrinsically tied to economic relations and relations of production. But power relations are what ultimately established this theater in which Western rationality and the rules of truth were played out.

M. Watanabe: In the first volume of *History of Sexuality, The Will to Knowledge*, you establish a distinction between statement and discourse. A discourse, especially a theoretical one, presumes and implies something that goes beyond the level of a statement.

M. Foucault: Yes. Precisely at that moment, while trying to do the history of scientific discourses, I studied Anglo-Saxon philosophy, analytical philosophy, a bit more closely. Analytical philosophy has made a host of remarkable observations that we can't ignore. My problem was somewhat different. My goal was not to try to understand how a statement came to exist or under what condition it could be true, but rather to consider entities greater than statements. Analyzing larger statements doesn't imply analyzing with any less rigor. The goal was to understand how a type of discourse can take shape and be governed by certain rules and how, if a statement doesn't abide by these rules, then it cannot belong to the discourse at all.

Let's take a very simple example. Until the end of the 18th century in France, there wasn't much difference between the discourse of a doctor and that of a charlatan. The differences were related to the success or failure of these discourses, to what someone had studied or not studied, but the nature of the things they said wasn't all that different. The type of discourse was almost the same. Then came a time when medical discourse was governed by a certain number of norms and rules which immediately told you not whether a doctor was good, but whether he was a doctor or a charlatan. Because he won't be saying the same things. He won't refer to the same type of causality or use the same concept. Again, this doesn't mean that someone can't imitate medical discourse perfectly well, without making errors, but not be a good doctor and so in fact be a charlatan. What I mean is that his discourse, in and of itself, will be governed by norms other than those of the charlatan. What must a medical discourse speak of, for example, in order to be a scientific discourse and be recognized as such? What concepts must it use, what type of theory must it refer to? These are the questions I was trying to answer in The Order of Things, or at least that I raised in The Order of Things and The Archaeology of Knowledge.

M. Watanabe: First we talked about space and power, and then about discourse and power. But in every series of interrogations, the pair of terms gives rise to the problem of the body. Since the '60s, the body has reemerged as an important element within theatrical practice, in the avant-garde theater that prioritized the body, the work of the body, the questioning of the actor's body. This phenomenon took on a global dimension. Theorists saw in this revalorization of the body a strategic antithesis to Western logocentrism. In Japan there was a cult of bodily practices that persisted within traditional culture. Some people of the avant-garde theater believed this cult was a perfect anchorage point for calling out the political and cultural alienation the Japanese had endured for three quarters of a century during the country's modernization and Westernization.

I won't repeat what we've already discussed quite a few times, but the technology of the body within traditional cultural practices, from martial arts to kabuki theater, likely set the stage for the modern training of the body, for the implementation of a series of disciplinary rules centered on what you call "the political technology of the body". Paradoxically, the more the military regime exploited the political technology of the body, the more the avant-garde Japanese theater became fascinated with the body and the knowledge of the body.

In your books, however, the body was present from the beginning: the great confinement was aimed at the bodily presence of the mad, and the clinic dealt with the bodies of the sick. But before Discipline and Punish, the body appeared only implicitly, and it's with this book about crime and correctional facilities that the body really made its spectacular debut.

M. Foucault: It did seem to me that there was something important about it, not only in the West's political and economic history, but also, one might say, in its metaphysical and philosophical history. How did I get to this by using relations of power as a starting point and retracing the history of the social sciences? How did Man become an object of inquiry and of concern—this is a classic question—but also an object of science, the kind that seeks specifically a knowledge of Man, what he consists of and the predictability of his behavior? So where do we search for this?

Here's where the question of space became key. The body is undoubtedly important in a feudal society. But how does the political, economic, and religious power exert itself over the body? I think this happens in three ways. First, we require that the body provide, generate, and disseminate signs: signs of respect, of devotion, of subjection and subservience. These signs are expressed through gestures and clothing. Second, the body is an object of power in that we're absolutely allowed to subject it to violence, and that includes death. This doesn't apply in every case and must be done according to certain rules, but the right to live and to die is one of the marks of sovereignty. Third, we can impose work.

That being said, power in a feudal society is indifferent to everything else: to whether people are in good health, to whether they reproduce, to how they live, behave, act, and work.

However, starting in the 17th century, a whole series of techniques were created with the goal of training and supervising people's physical behaviors. This was very clear in schools, for example. What was its purpose? To teach individuals a certain number of things. In schools, until the beginning of the 19th century, students shoved each other around in a little bunch around the teacher who stood in the middle, their eyes wide open, catching whatever words they wanted from the teacher's mouth. But from the 16th to the 19th century, a number of techniques were developed to teach people how to behave, how to act in a certain way. At this point, school also became a kind of physical training. More and more, students were required to form lines, to line up in front of the teacher, to ensure the headmaster could see what they were doing at every moment, whether they were distracted or not, whether they were listening, whether they were writing correctly during the dictation; all this was a training of the body. The same happened in the army: in the past, to be able to shoot with a bow and arrow, even badly, was enough. Then came learning how to shoot with a rifle, how to aim, exercises we spoke about earlier. The same went for the worker: you had the traditional craft of savoir faire, or methods of production, but eventually the terrorism of production-line work was imposed.

And so we realize, and here's the surprising part, that the political, economic, and cultural powers in Western societies had become focused on the body in a completely new way, in the form of a training, of surveillance, of performance, and of the intensification of performances. You had to do more and more in less and less time. I think the acceleration of the body's productivity was the historical condition under which the human sciences, sociology and psychology, were established. Hence a whole technology of the body, of which psychiatry eventually became a part in modern medicine.

This valorization of the body, not on a moral but on a political and economic level, was one of the fundamental attributes of the West. What's strange, however, is that this political and economic valorization of the body happened alongside an increasingly accentuated moral devaluation. The body was nothing, it was evil, it was what we were taught to cover, what we learned to become ashamed of. By the 19th century, before the so-called Victorian era, we had reached a kind of dissociation, a disjunction that was certainly at the origin of many individual psychological problems and maybe also larger collective and cultural ones: a body that was both economically over-valorized and a morally de-valorized.

M. Watanabe: As you explained yesterday in your seminar at the University of Tokyo, contrary to what we may believe, a negative attitude towards the body was not a Christian invention—a true platitude—it already existed among the Roman Stoics. Christianity introduced and generalized a technology of power centered around the body and sex, what you call "pastoral power".

M. Foucault: That's right.

M. Watanabe: Your comment about school reminds me of *Spring Awakening* by Wedekind that I saw at the Odeon a few years back. Is Wedekind's play not a sort of caricatural image of the Philanthropinum,[2] that you analyze in *The Will to Knowledge?*

M. Foucault: Absolutely. In German theater there is an entire tradition, which we know quite little about, of pedagogical theater. The school is the stage; you have Lenz's *The Professor* which is directly related to the Philanthropinum. Lenz based his text on pedagogical experiences of the 18th century, and unfortunately the French directors who staged it weren't aware of this. It was a play that was directly related to a kind of technique of that time: educational reform. A century later, Wedekind's *Spring Awakening* still raises the same problem.

M. Watanabe: Since Lenz's name was just mentioned, I'd like to talk about Patrice Chéreau, a young French director who got his start precisely with Lenz's *The Soldiers* about 15 years ago. Clearly tonight we won't escape the army and discipline. You told me that last year you saw *The Ring* staged by the Chéreau–Boulez team in Bayreuth. In *Spring Awakening*, which I alluded to earlier, there are also a few Wagner pieces used as elements for the production. As our discussion veers towards the Götterdämmerung, perhaps it's time for us to wrap up our conversation. But before we get to Wagner, would you speak to us a bit about your friends? Gilles Deleuze, for example, whose name was mentioned at the start of our interview, and Peter Klossowski, Georges Bataille, Maurice Blanchot, all those who shine throughout your books like magical constellations. Or Claude Mauriac who, in his private life, mentions a few unexpected Parisian intellectuals in his book *And How Hope is Violent* (1976), with a focus on their political activity—the inquiries you led on the illegal arresting of migrant workers or the actions of the Group of Information on Prisons. These are all very important personal testimonies about your work as an activist.

M. Foucault: So let's talk about friends, but not friends as friends. I come from a generation that is perhaps a bit old-fashioned, for whom friendship is something both essential and mysterious. And I must admit I always have a hard time integrating or assimilating these groups of friends into any type of organization, political group, school of thought, or academic circle; for me, friendship is kind of like a secret freemasonry. But it does have some visible aspects. You wanted to speak about Deleuze, who is of course someone who is very important to me. I believe he's the greatest French philosopher of our time.

M. Watanabe: "The next century will be Deleuzian"?

M. Foucault: Allow me to make a small correction. You have to imagine the controversial climate we live in in Paris. I remember very well in what sense I used that sentence. The sentence is actually as follows: at that time—this was in 1970—very few people know Deleuze, only a few insiders understand his importance, but maybe a day will come when "the century will be Deleuzian", with "century" taken in the Christian sense, the common understanding opposed to the elite, but this doesn't mean that Deleuze isn't an important philosopher. It's in the pejorative sense that I used the term "century". Yes, Deleuze is very important to me. Klossowski, Bataille, Blanchot were all very important to me. And I'm afraid I haven't sufficiently reflected their influence in my writing. I think this was out of shyness rather than ungratefulness. I say shyness because I believe their literary or philosophical work is so much more important than what I'm able to do that I don't think it's appropriate to valorize the little that I have done by placing it under the epigraph or sign of their names, as if to protect myself with some deity. And I don't want to protect myself, especially not through those I hold in too-high esteem to summon their patronage. These days, when I bring up the name Blanchot, students sometimes ask "who's that?"

M. Watanabe: It's that bad! That's outrageous!

M. Foucault: They know Klossowski a bit, Bataille too, but I started thinking that some of us, myself included, haven't been explicit enough about the debt we owe them. After all, in the '50s, these people were the first to save us from the Hegelian fascination we were trapped in, or at the very least that was hanging over us. Second, they were the first to raise the problem of the subject as fundamental for philosophy and modern thought. In other words, from Descartes to Sartre—and I don't mean to be controversial in saying this—it seems to me that the subject was something fundamental but also that we didn't address: it was something we didn't question. As a result, and as Lacan pointed out, Sartre never accepted the idea of the Freudian unconscious.

The idea that the subject isn't a basic and foundational entity, but rather the consequence of a series of processes—processes that aren't of the order of subjectivity but of something very difficult to name and bring to light, something even more fundamental and originary than the subject itself—never emerged in his thinking. The subject has an origin, a development, a history; the subject isn't something intrinsic. But who said this? Surely Freud, but Lacan was the one who showed it clearly, hence the importance of Lacan. In some sense Bataille, and also Blanchot and Klossowski in their own way, had dispelled the accepted idea of an originary subject by exposing forms of experience that shattered and even destroyed it, that pushed it to its limits and beyond, showing that, contrary to what philosophy had classically imputed to it, the subject didn't in fact have this intrinsic and self-sufficient form.

The commonality between all those we call structuralists is the subject's non-fundamental, non-intrinsic nature; it caused a lot of irritation among the previous generation and those representing it. In Lacan's psychoanalysis, in Lévi-Strauss' structuralism, in Barthes' analyses, in what Althusser did, in what I tried to do myself, in my own way, all of us agreed on the idea that we shouldn't start with the subject, the subject in the Cartesian sense, as the place from which everything else followed, that the subject itself had an origin. And that's how we rejoined Nietzsche.

M. Watanabe: I made the theater the main focus of our discussion, but in doing so I was not referring only to the theater as we practice it, but was also thinking precisely about Nietzsche, whose shadow seems to dominate our current thinking about the theater. In your beautiful text "Nietzsche, Genealogy, History", you insisted, as did Deleuze and Klossowski in their own writings, on the importance of the problem of the theater in Nietzsche's thought.

In this context, I'd like to come back to *The Ring* by Chéreau–Boulez, which you've seen. I myself had the chance to see and listen to it at the Festpielhaus' centenary in Bayreuth, and I intend to go back this year. We've already spoken about Chéreau's work and production of Marivaux's *The Dispute*, a fascinating work, which put Marivaux's play back in the historical and philosophical context of 18th-century France, where Rousseau and Sade would exchange thoughts about education, the training of the body, the soul, even the violence of the pedagogical gaze. And if my memory serves me well, the author of the prologue that Chéreau added in his production is someone you know well—it's François Regnault, who also collaborated on *The Ring* of the centenary?

M. Foucault: Yes, it's François Regnault. I've known him for ten years.

M. Watanabe: He's the brother of Anne Delbée, director of Claudel's *The Exchange*?

M. Foucault: That's right.

M. Watanabe: And what did you think of *The Ring*?

M. Foucault: I've known Boulez for a long time, since we're the same age and I met him when we were both 22, 23 years old. During that time, I was very interested in music. If I went to the Wagner cycle, it's certainly because Boulez invited me, but that's not the only reason. It's also because the work of Chéreau and Boulez was interesting on many levels. First, as it relates to *The Ring*, there was always a poor understanding of the theater's dramatic value in the West, and Wagner's work was reduced to its purely musical dimension. People listened to Wagner, but they didn't see Wagner. The goal of Wieland Wagner's beautiful productions was mostly to glorify the music and to serve as a kind of visual support for a music that, as Wagner wanted, played a secondary role in the sense that it found itself spatially below the production.

M. Watanabe: Whether we call it opera or musical drama, we have to admit: it's theater.

M. Foucault: That's it. Even though the music comes from below, it has to make its way onto a stage with visible characters. There doesn't even have to be this kind of screen between the audience and the stage, as is the case with classical opera.

But Chéreau saw this, and as if it was his calling, he did what the piece demanded of him. What's admirable is that Boulez, who is a great musician and conductor—if there are any at all these days—understood the task perfectly and accepted to play his part.

Second, and this is the whole problem of the anti-Hegelians of the 19th century like Wagner and Nietzsche who always played something of an ambiguous role in Western culture; Hegelianism had become so intrinsically tied to leftist thought that to be anti-Hegelian was to be right-wing! We're finally beginning to understand that, even though Nietzsche wrote some outright antisemitic things, this was not his case. What we're seeing now is that his thought cannot be labeled as purely right-wing. Wagner wasn't either. Whatever his disagreements with Nietzsche may have been, Wagner in fact tended towards anarchism; in any case his political thought was very different. And I think Chéreau did something very important when he understood this and allowed us to return to Wagner's interesting texts through his production; Wagner's theater isn't simply some kind of retrograde mythological declamation that supports and accompanies the beautiful music. They're important dramas that have historical meaning, something Chéreau demonstrated perfectly.

And third, Wagner, like Schopenhauer and Nietzsche, was one of the few to raise the question of the subject in non-Cartesian terms. He tried to understand how the Western concept of the subject was after all a limited one, and that it couldn't be used as an unconditional foundation for all forms of thought; and there's his encounter with the East. And I think that this dissolution of European subjectivity, of this restrictive subjectivity that our culture has imposed on us since the 19th century, is still very much at stake. Hence my interest in Zen Buddhism.

M. Watanabe: Indeed, I've heard that you're going to be spending a few days in a Zen monastery. We'll have to get back to the question of the body ...

M. Foucault: Precisely, in the history I'm trying to do of Western techniques of power, techniques that deal with the body, with people, with
behaviors, with people's souls, I was led to attribute a great deal of
importance to Christian discipline, to Christianity as something that
shaped Western individuality and subjectivity. I'd in fact love to compare these Christian techniques to those of Buddhist or far-eastern
spirituality, to compare these techniques which, to a certain extent,
have a lot in common. After all, Western and Christian monasticism
were influenced by and derived from Buddhist monasticism. But they
had a completely different effect since the rules of Buddhist spirituality are aimed at de-individualization, de-subjectification, at pushing
individuality to and beyond its limits for the sake of freeing the subject.
My project would be to explore some of this and to understand how,
through seemingly very similar techniques of asceticism, of meditation, through this overall resemblance, we get completely different
results. Probably because there were techniques for things that were
necessarily different. That's the first point, and truthfully the second
would be to find people in a far-eastern country who are also interested
in this type of problem so that we might conduct studies that are, if
not parallel, at least connected and in resonance with each other on the
discipline of the body and the formation of individuality.

M. Watanabe: As you know, Japanese spirituality was always expressed
through the body and the role of language in it was quite different with respect to Christian spirituality. That's one point. And then
in modern Japanese society, which was built on the 19th-century
Western model, modernization simply meant adopting the political,
economic, social, cultural norms of 19th-century Western society. The
Japanese were especially concerned with establishing the Cartesian,
Western subject. After the fascists' antiquated exploitation of the
body, the formation of the modern Westernized subject was seen as a
liberation with respect to imperial submission and an essential aspect
of the country's democratization. Hence the success of existentialism,
which had a longer lifespan in Japan than in France. But one also
wonders about the most important shortcoming in the formation of

modern individuality, which is that of Christianity. The problem you raise might shed some light on this sort of discrepancy, whose nature is not only historical but also cultural. You started your conference at the University of Tokyo yesterday with a comment about the double phenomenon that took place in the West in the 19th century on the subject of sexuality: the negation of our own desire, which is manifested as a kind of hysteria, and overabundance of sexual knowledge which allowed for different kinds of sexual sciences to emerge. In *The Will to Knowledge*, you insist on the importance of not misunderstanding the positive aspect of the political techniques of the body as a productive *dispositif* of knowledge about the body and sexuality; we had to undo the myth of what you called the "repressive hypothesis". Between the absence of discourse about sex, or the silence enforced on sex on the one hand, and the incitement of discourse about sex on the other, it's this second phenomenon that constitutes the fundamental element of the apparatus of power.

We unfortunately don't have time now to discuss the incitement of sexual discourse and censorship, which is still quite archaic and very much a Japanese phenomenon. However, in a society that sees itself as saturated with information and knowledge, what do you think is the role of the intellectual?

M. Foucault: I'd like to speak about this tomorrow at Asahi. I'll say briefly that it doesn't seem to me that these days an intellectual's role is to speak truths, to speak prophetic truths about the future. Maybe the diagnostician of the present, as I mentioned earlier, can try to help people grasp what is currently going on in domains where intellectuals might be competent. Through a small gesture that consists in shifting the gaze, the intellectual makes visible what is visible, reveals what is so close, so immediate, so intimately linked to who we are that we aren't able to see it. This role is much closer to that of what was called the "philosopher" in the 18th century.

M. Watanabe: This is what you call the specific intellectual as opposed to the universal one.

M. Foucault: That's right. There are things happening now in the organization of health, in censorship, in the liberation of sexuality, the environment or ecology. There's a whole series of events where I think the intellectual is competent; the atomic physicist, the biologist for the environment, the doctor for medicine have to intervene to help us understand what's going on, to diagnose it, to predict the dangers, and not simply to make a systematic, unconditional, global judgment.

I think that knowledge in our societies has become something so vast and complex that it is in fact becoming the unconscious of our societies. We don't know what we know, we don't know what the different effects of knowledge are; so it seems to me that the intellectual can have the role of transforming this unconscious knowledge that rules over our society into something conscious.

M. Watanabe: With this displacement of the gaze and the ethical role it plays, our dialogue has ended, after a spiraling trajectory, back where we started, with our reflections on the gaze in philosophy and in the theater. Thank you very much.

Translated by Alexia Trigo

NOTES

1 In *Critique*, no. 343, December 1975, pp. 1207–1227.
2 Allusion to a sexual education party organized by Basedow in 1776 in his philanthropic college.

7

METHODOLOGY FOR A KNOWLEDGE OF THE WORLD

How to Get Rid of Marxism

"Sekai-ninshiki no hōhō: Marx shugi wo dō shimatsu suru ka" ("La méthodologie pour la connaissance du monde: comment se débarrasser du marxisme"), interview with R. Yoshimoto on April 25, 1977, in Umi, July 1978, pp. 302–328.

Dits et écrits III, no. 235

R. Yoshimoto: Since today I have the opportunity of meeting you, I'd like to interview you about what, among my own areas of interest, is likely to retain your attention, and which thus might constitute a point of contact between us. By which I mean I will leave it at that. As regards particular themes, I think, in spite of everything, that it's difficult to find a meeting ground. So I would like to interview you about what might best bring us together.

DOI: 10.4324/9781003303763-9

M. Foucault: I have heard about you and your name has been mentioned frequently in conversation. So I'm very happy and honored to meet you today. Unfortunately, since your writings have been translated neither into French nor into English, I haven't had the opportunity to read your work firsthand, but I thought to myself, surely I must have some common points of interest with you, for M. Hasumi gave me a sort of résumé of your work and provided some commentary. There are things on which I would like to have some clarification, and it seemed to me that we share two or three areas of interest. Of course, I take no credit for this, but clearly, we do deal with similar themes. I too intend to ask you some questions. I'm afraid however that they will be fairly summary in nature, and I beg you not to hold this against me.

R. Yoshimoto: Reading your works, *The Order of Things* in particular, I tried to locate a point of contact, something that interests me at the moment and that encompasses a range of issues. I thought of the following theme, even if it can be formulated in different ways: how to get rid of Marxism? Or, how not to get rid of it? It's a question I have been thinking about, and that I'm having some difficulty elucidating, at this very moment. You touched upon Marxism in a passage in *The Order of Things*. You say something like this: Marxism put forward, within the framework of 19th-century thought, a problematic that conflicts with bourgeois or classical economy; this problematic fits seamlessly into the intellectual model of the 19th century. In 19th-century thought, Marxism is like a fish in water; outside of it, it stops breathing. Marxism professes to change the world, but it does not have the wherewithal to do so; in short, Marxism is perfectly integrated into 19th-century thought. It is this passage that caught my interest. In parallel with this, you mention the most important contributions made by 19th-century thought, including by Marxism. First of all, it highlighted the historicity of economy. Then—I am not sure if I have got this right—it raised the problem of the limits of the value of human work. Lastly, it set a term for the end of history. And you assert that these are the problems the 19th century raised and which continue to preoccupy posterity.

The question I ask myself right now is: can one or can one not get rid of Marxism? I understand how you have proceeded. For me it's a bit different. And it's on this topic that I'd like us to exchange a few ideas. Something else interested me. Marxism fits perfectly, to use your terms, into the archeological tendency of a totalizing thought, and in no way goes beyond it. This is a very exciting point of view, and I am in complete agreement. But for me this doesn't constitute a flaw in Marxism or in Marx's thought, but a quality. That Marxism or Marx's thought are continuous with classical economy, without having gotten rid of it, isn't that rather something positive? In other words, it seems to me that if, even today, Marx's thought offers possibilities, it's because it did not get rid of classical economy.

I think there are certain nuances that differentiate Marx's thinking from that of his colleague Engels. To sum up schematically Marx's thought, at its base there is a philosophy of nature, then above this is an historical analysis (in terms of the history of nature) of the social and economic structure, and finally at the top is the whole domain of the Hegelian theory of will. Hegel understood by this a whole set of things, whether it concerns right, the State, religion, civil society, and of course morality, the person, and self-consciousness. Now it seems to me that Marx considered this whole domain of the Hegelian theory of will as resting upon an analysis of society conducted in terms of the history of nature. This treatment means that Marx did not get rid of Hegel. He neither eliminated nor excluded him, but preserved him intact as an object of analysis. In my view, things are a little different with Engels. In Engels, we have at the base the concept of the history of nature, and above it the history of society. I think that Engels was of the opinion that the set of domains covered under the Hegelian theory of will could come later. By proceeding this way, Engels artfully got rid of Hegel. That is to say, he considered that all these problems—the individual will, self-consciousness, individual ethics or morals—were negligible as drivers of history. For Engels, history was moved by an entire people or by the class wills that made it up. He must have told himself that individual wills did not deserve any attention, and he could safely dispense with them.

So, unlike Marx, Engels skillfully reorganized *The Phenomenology of Spirit* by separating what concerns individuals from what concerns the community. As for the determining factor of history, he reckoned that will or individual morality, which is to say personal morality, could be ignored, on the pretext that it is a totally aleatory factor. For me the fact that Marx did not get rid of Hegel, and that he kept as is Hegel's attempt at a system of the theory of will, always seemed to me to be an important problem.

I never stop wondering: isn't the way in which Engels makes a complete break with Hegel a flaw at some level? And how can we overcome this flaw and apply it to our epoch? It struck me as important to separate this domain of the theory of will into three levels. First, what I will call the domain of individual phantasm, then the (sociological and ethnological) domain of the family, kinship, and sex, that is to say the dual phantasm, and finally the domain that covers the collective phantasm. The idea is that by separating them out in this way we might be able to build on the part of Hegel that Marx did not want to evacuate. That's how I have tried to deepen the question.

It's on this topic that I would like to question you. When it comes to knowing what problem remains once one has gotten rid of Marx, I believe you have completely excluded the whole territory covered by the Hegelian theory of will from general consideration, in other words from the methodology for a knowledge of the world. And once you eliminated it from your overall conception, you considered that these were all particular problems, channeling your research towards the history of punishment or the history of madness. It seems to me that in this way you have excluded from your overall conception the Hegelian theory of will by completely transforming this domain—which for Hegel constituted a huge inquiry—into individual themes.

On another note, there's something I found quite characteristic when reading *The Order of Things*. I wondered if you hadn't totally denied the method that consists in finding a kernel of meaning behind an expression, or in words, and if you had not presented this negating attitude as a problem. I suppose this problematic comes from Nietzsche. On the question of knowing if history has a cause and an effect, and if human will is actualizable, Nietzsche explains that the notion according to which a cause produces an effect is possible only at a semiological level, that history itself has neither cause nor effect, and that there is no link between cause and effect. I think that Nietzsche is suggesting that history is due to chance, that it is a sequence of events produced by chance and involving neither a concept of progress nor regularity. It seems to me that your approach is similar to his. For my part, I seek to preserve the domain of the Hegelian theory of will and, in so doing, to get closer to Marx, which is to say to the historical laws of society, whereas you seem to have gotten rid of them completely. After which, among the innumerable series of problems that come about by chance, without cause, effect, or link between them, you single out one which might give you an approach to history. I take it that's your idea. I would be very happy to hear a more extensive analysis of this subject and I think it would be very instructive for me.

M. Foucault: Rather than respond to you globally, since you have broached several questions it seems to me preferable to consider them one after the other. First of all, I am extremely happy and grateful to know that my books have been read and understood so deeply. What you have just said illustrates perfectly the depth of this reading. It is true moreover that whenever I go back to this book, I feel a kind of regret. If I were writing The Order of Things now, the book would take another form. I now have another way of reasoning. It's a rather abstract essay, and limited to logical considerations. Whereas personally I am strongly attracted to concrete problems, such as psychiatry or the prison for example. I now believe that it's by starting from these concrete problems that one can generate something. So, what needs to be brought to light by starting out with these concrete problems? It's what we should call a "new political imaginary". What I'm interested in is bringing about this new political imagination. What characterizes our generation—it's probably the same for the one that precedes us and the one that follows us—is, without any doubt, a lack of political imagination. What does this mean? For example, the men of the 18th century and the men of the 19th century at least had the ability to dream the future of human society. Their imagination was not to be outdone on this sort of question: what is it to live as a member of this community? Or, what are social and human relations? Indeed, from Rousseau to Locke or to those known as the utopian socialists, one might say that humanity, or rather Western society, was teeming with fertile outcomes of the socio-political imagination.

Whereas today, with us, there is such an aridity of political imagination! It's hard not to be surprised at this poverty. In this sense, we are the complete opposite of the men of the 18th and 19th centuries. It is nonetheless possible to understand the past by analyzing the present. But when it comes to political imagination, we have to acknowledge that we are living in a very impoverished world. When we look for where this poverty of imagination on the socio-political level in the 20th century comes from, it seems to me, after all, that Marxism plays an important part. That's why I discuss Marxism. So you can see that the theme "How to get rid of Marxism", which serves in some sense as a connecting thread for the question you have asked me, is also fundamental for my thinking. One thing is certain: that Marxism has contributed and continues to contribute to this impoverishment of the political imagination. This is our starting point.

Your reasoning starts out from the idea that we have to distinguish Marx, on the one hand, Marxism on the other, as an object we have to get rid of. I am in complete agreement with you. I wouldn't find it very appropriate to do away with Marx himself. Marx is unquestionably a human being, a person who unerringly expressed certain things, in other words he is an undeniable being in terms of historical event. By definition one cannot suppress such an event. Just as, for example, the Naval Battle of the Sea of Japan, in the Tsushima Strait, is an event that actually took place, Marx is a fact one cannot suppress. To transcend him would be as senseless as denying the Naval Battle of the Sea of Japan.

The situation is totally different as far as Marxism is concerned. That's because Marxism is the cause of the impoverishment, the desiccation of the political imagination that I was speaking about a moment ago. To really reflect on this, one must bear in mind that Marxism is nothing other than a mode of power, in an elementary sense. In other words, Marxism is a sum of power relations or a sum of mechanisms and dynamics of power. On this point we should analyze how Marxism functions in modern society. This is a necessary task, just as for past societies one analyzed the role played by scholastic philosophy or Confucianism. The difference being that in our case Marxism was not born of morals or a moral principle like scholastic philosophy or Confucianism. The case of Marxism is more complex, because it's something that emerged, within rational thought, as a science. As for knowing what types of power relations a so-called "rational" society can assign to science, this cannot be reduced to the idea that science functions only as a sum of propositions taken for the truth. It is at the same time something intrinsically linked to a whole series of coercive propositions. Which is to say that Marxism as science—to the extent that it is a science of history, of the history of humanity—is a dynamic of coercive effects, concerning a certain truth. Its discourse is a prophetic science that diffuses a coercive force over a certain truth, not only in the direction of the past, but toward the future of humanity. In other words, what's important is that historicity and the prophetic character function as coercive forces concerning truth.

Then there is another characteristic. Marxism has never been able to exist without a political movement, be it in Europe or elsewhere. I say political movement, but more exactly, Marxism has been unable to function without the existence of a political party. The fact that Marxism has been unable to function without the existence of a State that needed it as a philosophy is a rare phenomenon that never before appeared in the world or in Western society. Today, certain countries function as States only by availing themselves of this philosophy, but there are no precedents for this in the West. The States from before the French Revolution were always based on religion. But those after the Revolution founded themselves on what we call philosophy, which is a radically new and surprising form that had never existed before, at least in the West. Naturally, prior to the 18th century, there had never been an atheist State. The State was necessarily founded on religion. Consequently, there could never be a philosophical State. Then, beginning around the time of the French Revolution, different political systems, explicitly or implicitly, started to go in search of a philosophy. I think that this is a truly important phenomenon. It goes without saying that such a philosophy splits in two, and its power relations get caught up in the dynamic of state mechanisms. To sum all this up, the three aspects of Marxism—Marxism as scientific discourse, Marxism as prophesy, Marxism as State philosophy or class ideology—are inevitably intrinsically linked to the whole set of power relations. If the problem of knowing whether or not to get rid of Marxism is raised, is it not at the level of the power dynamic formed by these aspects of Marxism? Marxism, viewed from this perspective, is today going to be called into question. The problem is less about telling ourselves that it is necessary to free ourselves from this type of Marxism than of throwing off the dynamic of power relations linked to a Marxism that performs those particular functions.

If I may, I'd like to add two or three things by way of conclusion. If the real problem is as I have just stated, the question of the method that corresponds to it is just as important. In defining the problem, an essential one for me, of how to move beyond Marxism, I have tried not to fall into the trap of traditional solutions. There are two traditional ways of confronting this problem. One is academic, the other is political. But whether it is from an academic or a political point of view, in France the problem unfolds broadly in the following way. Either one critiques the propositions of Marx himself, saying: "Marx puts forward such and such a proposition. It is true or not? Contradictory or not? Is it premonitory or not?" Or else one develops a critique of the following sort: "In what way does Marxism today betray what would have been reality for Marx?" I find both of these traditional critiques ineffective. In the final count they are points of view that are captive of what we can call the force of truth and its effects: what is true, and what is not true? In other words, the question "What is the true and authentic Marx?", the kind of perspective that consists in wondering about the link between truth effects and the State philosophy that is Marxism, impoverishes our thought.

On the topic of these traditional points of view, the position I want to take now is completely other. I will succinctly say three things on this matter.

Firstly, as I said to you a moment ago, Marx is a historical existence, and from this point of view he is simply one of the faces of history, the same as any other historical existence. And Marx's face clearly belongs to the 19th century. In the 19th century Marx played a particular, almost determining role. But this role is clearly typical of the 19th century and it functions only there. Bringing this fact to light requires attenuating the power relations linked to Marx's prophetic character. At the same time, Marx definitely articulated a certain type of truth, which prompts us to ask if his words are universally true or not, of what kind of truth was he the bearer, and if in bringing forth this absolute truth he paved the way for a deterministic historiology. This kind of debate is to be avoided. In demonstrating that Marx ought not to be considered a decisive bearer of truth, it seems necessary to attenuate or reduce the effect that Marxism exerts as a modality of power.

A second problem I'd like to bring up is the need to attenuate or reduce the power relations that Marxism exhibits in its relationships with a party, which is to say as the expression of a political bias. This point entails the following requirement. Since Marxism functioned only as the expression of a political party, it follows that various important problems that occur in real society are swept from the political horizon. The need to bring all these excluded problems to the surface is pressing. In Marxist parties, as well as in traditional Marxist discourses, what was lacking was the ability to take into consideration all these problems, for example medicine, sexuality, reason, madness.

Moreover, in order to reduce the modalities of power linked to Marxism as the expression of a political party, all these new problems I just named—medicine, sexuality, reason, madness—will have to be brought together with various social movements, whether these be protests or revolts. Political parties tend to ignore these social movements and even to weaken their force. From this perspective, the importance of all these movements is clear to me. All these movements start with intellectuals, with students, with prisoners, with what is called the *Lumpenproletariat*. It's not that I acknowledge an absolute value in their movement, but I nonetheless believe it is possible, at once on the logical and the political levels, to recover what has been monopolized by Marxism and by Marxist parties. In addition, when one thinks of the critical activities going on every day in the countries of eastern Europe, the need to be done with Marxism seems obvious to me, be it in the Soviet Union or elsewhere. In other words, we see here the element that allows us to move beyond Marxism as State philosophy.

I think with that I have now managed to sketch out the horizon as I see it. Now I would like to ask you what direction you are taking, setting aside all traditional, academic, and political directions, as regards the question: how to be done with Marxism, how to move beyond it?

But I have perhaps not yet adequately answered your question. The problems you raised include important points, for example, Nietzsche, the kernel of meaning, the question of knowing if everything happens without a cause or not, and also the problem of the phantasm and of individual will in the context of the 19th century—I understand that this is an essential aspect of your own problematic. You spoke about individual will, referring to the difference between Marx and Engels as concerns Hegel. You ask an important question: is there not precisely a possibility remaining in the fact that at the level of individual will Marx did not overturn Hegel as radically as Engels did? I'm not sure I'm able to answer you fully. But I'll give it a try. It's a very difficult problem for us Westerners. For, in the past, Western philosophy has barely talked about the will. Obviously, Western philosophy has talked about consciousness, desire, about passions, but the mention must be, I think, the greatest weakness of Western philosophy.

To my mind, if Western philosophy has dealt with will up to this point it's been in only two ways. On one hand, on the model of natural philosophy, and on the other on the model of philosophy of right. In other words, will is force, on the model of natural philosophy, which can be represented by Leibniz. If one follows the model of the philosophy of right, will is a purely moral question, namely the individual consciousness of good and evil, which is represented by Kant. Either one reasons in terms of will-nature-force, or one reasons in terms of will-right-good and evil. In any event, Western philosophy's reflection on the question of will comes down to these two schemas.

Now this schema for thinking about will, meaning the traditional schema of nature and right, experienced a break. I think we can situate that break at the beginning of the 19th century. Well before Marx, a break with the tradition had clearly taken place. This event has somewhat fallen into oblivion in the West today, but we still fear it, and the more I think about it the more I think it's important: I am talking about Schopenhauer. Naturally, Marx couldn't read Schopenhauer. But it was none other than Schopenhauer who introduced into Western philosophy the question of will, by way of various comparisons with Eastern philosophy. For Western philosophy to rethink the question of will independently of the perspectives of nature and right, there had to be an intellectual clash between the West and the East. But one cannot say—far from it—that the problem has been taken very far in that direction. It goes without saying that Schopenhauer's point of view was taken up by Nietzsche, who came up just a moment ago. In this context, for Nietzsche, will was in some sense a principle of intellectual decipherment, a principle of comprehension—even if it was not absolute—for defining reality. You see, he thought that by starting from will, one could go on to grasp the couple will-passion, or will-phantasm. Will to know, will to power. All this completely subverted the traditional concept of will in the West. He didn't merely subvert the concept of will; one could say that he subverted the relations between knowledge, the passions, and will.

But frankly, the situation was not completely subverted. It's possible that it remained just as before. Later, Nietzsche, Husserlian philosophy, the existentialist philosophers, Heidegger, all those people, Heidegger in particular, tried to elucidate the problem of will, but they never managed to define clearly the method that would have allowed them to analyze the phenomenon from the perspective of will. In short, Western philosophy has always been incapable of thinking the question of will in a relevant way.

We now need to ask ourselves under what form we can think the problem of will. I said a moment ago that up to now, in order to address the relations between human action and will, the West has had only two methods. In brief, from a methodological as well as a conceptual point of view, the question has been addressed only along traditional lines: nature–force or right–good and evil. But oddly, to think about will, no one thought to borrow a method from military strategy. It seems to me that the question of will can be framed in terms of struggle, in other words from a strategic point of view as a way to analyze conflict whenever various antagonisms arise.

For example, it's not that everything occurs without a reason, and it's not that everything occurs according to causality, whenever something happens in the domain of nature. But it's by declaring that what makes the historical events of humanity or human actions decipherable is a strategic point of view, as a principle of conflict and struggle, that we can tackle the rational point of view of a type we have yet to define. Once we have established this point of view, the fundamental concepts it will be helpful to deploy are strategy, conflict, struggle, and incidents. What the use of these concepts can clarify is the antagonism in any situation where adversaries face off, a situation where one wins and the other loses, namely the incident. Now, an overview of Western philosophy shows that neither the concept of the incident, nor the method of analysis borrowed from the strategy, nor the notions of antagonism, struggle, and conflict have been adequately thought through. Consequently, the new possibility for intellectual deciphering that philosophy today must offer consists in the ensemble of concepts and methods of the strategic point of view. I say "must", but that simply means we have to try to go in this direction, even if it's possible we will fail. In any case we have to try.

One might say that this endeavor engages in Nietzschean genealogy. But it would have to involve a reworked content, theoretically enhanced by the solemn and mysterious concept of "will to power", and at the same time it will require finding a content that corresponds better to reality than Nietzsche.

I'd like to add a footnote to what I have just said. There is a term that Marx obviously used, but which today is taken as being almost obsolete. It's the term "class struggle". When one adopts the point of view I just described, does it not then become possible to rethink this term? For example, Marx says, essentially, that the motor of history resides in class struggle. And many after him have repeated this thesis. Indeed, it's an undeniable fact. Sociologists endlessly revive the debate in order to define what a class is and who belongs to it. But up to now no one has examined or investigated the question of what struggle is. What is struggle, when one says "class struggle"? Since we say "struggle", it's a matter of conflict and of war. But how does this war unfold? What is its objective? What are its means? Upon what rational qualities does it rest? What I'd like to discuss, taking off from Marx, is not the problem of the sociology of class, but the strategic method concerning struggle. That's where my interest in Marx is anchored, and it is from there that I would like to raise questions.

Now, around me struggles are occurring and evolving in the form of multiple movements. For example, the problem of Narita,[1] or the struggle that you led in the square in front of Parliament against the US–Japan Security Treaty in 1960. There are struggles in France and in Italy as well. These struggles, to the extent that they are battles, enter into my analysis. For example, in order to reflect on the problems raised by these struggles, the Communist Party never deals with struggle itself. All it asks is: "To what class do you belong? Are you leading this struggle as a representative of the proletarian class?" It is distinctly not a question about the strategic aspect, namely: what is struggle? My interest is in the incidences of the antagonisms themselves: who gets involved in the struggle? With what and how? Why is this struggle happening? What is its basis? I have not had the opportunity to read your books, but I have heard a lot about your practical activities and your work. I would therefore be very interested in hearing your opinion on what I have just said.

R. Yoshimoto: In what you have just said there are some points where I feel I can take the question further. By which I mean that I can propose other interpretations. On one hand, you evoked the problem of will in Nietzsche and Marx, then you defined it in relation to struggle in the sense of "class struggle", and finally you raised a series of problems related to current events. I'd like to delve deeper into all these points. I can suggest some alternative points of view, after which I'd like to ask you some more questions.

At the outset, you said we must distinguish between Marx's thought and Marxism, to the extent that Marx is a being who existed in an historical and classical past. I too have always said that Marx the man was different from Marxism. So I am entirely in agreement with you on this. I understand this viewpoint very well.

As far as Marx's prophetic tone is concerned, his prophecy might be summed up as follows: the classes will disappear, as well as the State. In this regard, there are States which have Marxism as their philosophy. There are some in Europe just as there are in China and Soviet Russia. These countries are absolutely not seeking to dismantle the philosophical State; moreover it is by not dismantling it that they exercise power. To borrow the expression you just used, this leads to a considerable impoverishment of the political imagination of the moment. On this topic, if, instead of saying, "It's precisely for this reason that one can liquidate Marxism!" one were to come to its defense, here is what one might say: the State will one day disappear, as well as the classes. Today these exist in a temporary form, before they disappear. It's basically a temporary problem and we can accept it as a temporary form. Simply, what is not acceptable is the type of power that consists in substantializing a State that is merely a temporary form, by dwelling on it and making of it a mode of domination. Socialist States seem indeed to be in this category, and to have settled on this direction more than ever. However, it seems to me that the philosophy of the State—or the philosophical State—that exists in actual fact in a temporary form and the negation of the very principle of that philosophy are not of the same nature.

I have always believed that one can distinguish between the fact that a philosophy actualizes itself in a provisional State and the fact of rejecting a philosophy that effectively dominates the State, that is no longer anything but a self-justifying mode of power. Moreover, what you expressed globally on this point seems to me to come down to this: the very fact of asking the question of the right way to understand

Marx already participates in the current impoverishment of the political imagination, and it's a problem that has been settled long ago. On this point I have some reservations and I can't go along with you. I think we must rigorously distinguish what stems from principle from the modalities of power that really exist in Marxist States. It seems to me that these are two different things. The problem is not the fact that Marxism built its power on a State philosophy or on a philosophical State; it's above all a problem of ideas. In history, the sum of individual wills and practical realizations does not necessarily appear as a motor of society. Why does history always seem to be founded on chance, and why does it appear as a failure of ideas? It seems to me we should delve deeper, beyond Marxism, into the problem of why history seems to have no relation to individual will. Now, the sum of individual wills includes, to speak like Hegel, morality and practical ethics. Eliminating this problem completely by reducing it to the general will, or the will of the classes, has this not produced something philosophically inadequate? Doesn't the problem stem from the fact that the sum of individual wills installed in power, and the will that manifests itself as total power, appear as being entirely different? Might we not pursue this point, as a principle? To take things a little further, it seems to me that the idea that the development of history is determined only by chance is questionable.

Let me explain. That would mean that an infinite sequence of chances creates a necessity. And if we admit that chance always includes necessity, the question of knowing if history is determined by chance or by necessity comes down to defining the limit-point at which a sequence of chances is transformed into necessity. It then seems to me that instead of getting rid of it, as you do on the grounds that it impoverishes politics, Marx's philosophical and historical prophecy remains valid.

I therefore have trouble accepting Nietzsche's idea that history is determined only by chance and that there is neither necessity nor causality involved. In my opinion, Nietzsche had a fairly cursory vision of the relation between chance and necessity. He let himself be guided by his intuition, or rather by questions of sensibility. We will need to think a bit more about this problem of the relation between chance and necessity. And it is on this score that Marx's thinking can remain a political model, both living and real. Your work leads me to believe that we need to dig a bit deeper into this problem of chance and necessity, and of the limit-point at which a sequence of chances is transformed into necessity, along with the problem of the scope and the territory of this transformation. It's on this topic that I would like to as you some questions.

As for the theory of will, I fear that unless I recapitulate for you the history of Marxism in Japan since the Second World War you will have difficulty understanding how the theory of will can include problems that range from the philosophy of the State to religion, ethics, self-consciousness. Postwar Japanese Marxism tried to revive the skeletal framework of Hegel that Marx had not rejected—we call this "subjective materialism"—while molding it in conformity with the Marxist materialism that had developed in Russia. I think this is diametrically opposed to the approach adopted by French Marxism. Japanese subjective Marxism tried to revive whole swaths of Hegel—the philosophy of the State, the theory of religion, individual morality, and even self-consciousness—incorporating them fully into Marxism. It is via this movement that we sought to synthesize the entire Hegelian system under the form of the theory of will.

If I were to take this question in the direction you have suggested, it might lead us too far astray. I'd prefer instead to lay out my position a bit more precisely. In the evolution of materialism in Japan since the war, or rather beyond this evolution, I tried to consider the domain of the theory of will as the inner determination of practical consciousness in the manner of Hegel. And I attempted to circumvent the ethical theme, which appears to be unresolved, by dividing the whole of this territory into three: that of communal will, that of dual will, and that of individual will.

A moment ago, you said that when we evoke class struggle in Marx, we should not place the accent on class, but rather try to resolve the problem of struggle from the perspective of will. You asked yourself: who is fighting against whom? How? With whom is it just to fight? And you added that these are pressing questions in these times. I think I could develop all this in my own way, but I also tell myself that, before getting into that, Marxism would have to first resolve the issue of how it got rid of the problems of dual will and individual will by shifting the meaning of class struggle in the direction of communal will as the motor force of history. Moreover, in Japanese Marxism, in its development and in discussions of it, the definition of the concept of class struggle is not the same as it is, for example, in Althusser in France or Lukács in Germany. When we say class, we are certain that it has to be defined on a socioeconomic basis and that it must be defined as an idea. I have always believed that class encompasses two problems: the problem of the idea, and the problem of the real and social.

This is why I deemed it necessary to examine first of all the concept of class. I imagine the concept developed differently in European Marxism. As regards concrete problems, I'd like to bring up the ten years preceding the Second World War, the war itself, and the ten years that followed, in other words all of postwar history. I wonder if the determination of nature by way of the will to power in Nietzsche and the determination of the natural state in the sense popularized by Engels are so far from. one another. Nietzsche considered history a process whereby men are moved by a will to power that surpasses them. In the natural state, men suffer war, violence, disorder, death etc., all of which Nietzsche considers to be part of human nature. He believes that when all this nature comes to be repressed, that's when conscience and human morality appear. That is why he viewed human nature from the perspective of biological *Leben*. Engels placed the ideal state a bit higher than the determination of nature, namely in the gregarious life of primitive communism. I think such a State never existed. In my opinion, Engels thought that this ideal constituted at once the origin and the end. These two ways of thinking are represented, if I may refer to my own intellectual experience from the Second World War, in imperial militarism in Japan and in the intellectual manifestations of fascism and Stalinism, which are not fundamentally different from one another. Our problematic lay in the realization that these two ways of thinking were not really different and that they both had to be rejected.

If we situate the objective of the struggle you mention, in the sense in which we speak of "class struggle", in facts, I fear that inevitably this struggle is completely isolated. I think that this is the case in Japan, and probably everywhere else in the world. When we ask ourselves what we are struggling against, it's not only against capitalism, it's also against socialism. Thus, the problem follows reality around everywhere, and necessarily it ends up being an isolated struggle in the world. We can count on nothing, and we are inevitably backed into a corner. Yet if we try to elaborate this as an intellectual or philosophical problem, there too we find ourselves completely cut off from the world. In short, I wonder if it is not our fate to be backed into a corner. My thoughts on this topic are increasingly pessimistic.

I would like to ask you about this. Nietzsche rejected the entire domain covered by the Hegelian theory of will, taxing it with being a vile concept that represses human nature, and I have the impression that in a similar way you develop your method after having skillfully wiped the slate clean of the isolation, the solitude, the passions, or the darkness that Nietzsche rejected, or of all sorts of other things: rigidity, for example. On the contrary, you seem to deal skillfully with relations between things at a level close to structurally similar concepts in algebra, that is to say, things, virtual facts. And, in so doing, I have the impression that you ward off the sort of feeling of isolation in the world that I experience personally. I'd like to ask you about that.

M. Foucault: I sense that you have just raised a new problem with these reservations about what I have said. But I am fundamentally in agreement with you. I feel at one with you on your reservations, more than with your ideas. Among the questions, the first was something like this: can one be done with Marxism for the simple reason that it has been intimately linked to state power relations? Can we not go a bit deeper into this question? I'd like to respond as follows, although this is less an answer than a proposition, but I'd like to present it in a somewhat brutal fashion.

As long as one considers Marxism as the ensemble of modes of manifesting power that is linked, one way or another, to the word of Marx,

I think that the least one can expect of anyone living in the second half of the 20th century is that they examine systematically each one of these modes of manifestation. We suffer this power today in passivity, or in fear, or out of interest, but we need to free ourselves from it completely. That's something we must systematically examine, with the real feeling of being completely free in relation to Marx.

Of course, to be free in relation to Marxism does not mean going back to the source to find out what Marx actually said, to grasp his word in its pure state and accept it as law. Nor does it mean revealing, for instance, using the Althusserian method, how the true word of the prophet Marx has been misinterpreted. What's important does not lie in this kind of question about form. But as I said to you, re-checking one by one the entirety of the functions of the modes of manifestation of power linked to the word of Marx himself seems to me to represent a worthwhile effort. There then arises, of course, the problem of knowing how to think about prophesy.

Personally, what attracts me in Marx's writings are the historical works, the essay on the coup d'état of Louis-Napoléon Bonaparte or on class struggle in France or on the Commune. Reading these historical works calls attention to two things. The analyses Marx carries out there, even if we can't consider all of them to be completely accurate, be it in regard to the context, the antagonisms of the relations, the strategy, or the links of interest, unquestionably far surpass those of his contemporaries in their perceptiveness, their effectiveness, their analytic quality and, at any rate, they radically surpass all previous research.

Now the analyses in the historical work always end with some prophetic words. These were prophesies about a near future, short-term prophesies—about the coming year or the coming month. But one can say that Marx's prophesies were almost all false. Analyzing the situation in 1851 to 52, just after the coup d'état, he says that the collapse of the Empire is near. He talks about the end of the capitalist system and is mistaken about the demise of bourgeois dictatorship. What does all that mean? Analyses of rare intelligence, and yet the facts that they announce are immediately belied by reality. Why?

Here's what I think. It seems to me that what we find in Marx's work is, in some sense, a play between the formation of a prophesy and the definition of a target. The socialist discourse of the epoch was made up of two concepts, but was unable to distinguish them sufficiently. On the one hand, a historical consciousness, or the consciousness of historical necessity, or at any rate the idea that in the future one thing or another prophetically must come to pass. On the other hand, a discourse of struggle—a discourse, we might say, that stems from the theory of will—the goal of which is to identify a target to attack. In actual fact, the fall of Napoléon III was less a prophesy than an objective to be attained by proletarian struggle. But the two discourses—the consciousness of historical necessity, or the prophetic aspect, and the goal of struggle—were unable to play out to the end. This can apply to the long-term prophesies. For example, the notion that the State will disappear is erroneous. As for me, I don't think that what is happening concretely in socialist countries points towards the realization of this prophesy. But as soon as the disappearance of the State is defined as an objective, Marx's words take on unprecedented reality. Undeniably, we are witnessing a hypertrophy of power or an excess of power in socialist countries as in capitalist countries. And I think that the reality of these mechanisms of power, which are of gigantic complexity, justifies, from the strategic viewpoint of a struggle of resistance, the disappearance of the State as an objective.

Now then, let's get back to your two questions. They concern, on the one hand, the relation between necessity and chance in history, and on the other the theory of will. I have already spoken briefly about historical necessity, but what interests me primarily is what you had to say about the evolution of Japanese Marxism after the war, about its specific nature, and about the place the theory of will occupies in it.

I think that this is a fundamental problem. I would like to argue in the same vein as you, at least to the extent that I have understood you. The way of thinking that consists in approaching will from this perspective is essential. It really did not exist at all in the mind of the average Frenchman that I am. In any event, it is indeed clear that the tradition of French Marxism has overlooked the analysis of the different levels of will, as well as the perspective on the specifics of their three foundations. The fact is that this domain remains completely unexplored in the West. It seems necessary to me to bring to light the reason that the importance of the problem of will has been neither understood nor analyzed.

To do so, we need to think about the existence of an organization by the name of the Communist Party. It has been a determining factor in the history of Western Marxism. Yet it has never been extensively analyzed. It is an organization without precedent. It cannot be compared to anything else; it does not function in modern society along the lines of the Radical Party or the Social Democratic Party. It's not simply a group of individuals who share the same opinion and participate in the same struggle towards the same end. It's a more complex organization. This is an overused metaphor, and I don't mean to sound malicious, but its organization inevitably makes one think of a monastic order. There has been no end to the discussion about the nature of this party. In relation to class struggle, to the revolution, what is its goal, what should its role be, its function? Everyone knows that all these problems were at the center of its debates. The polemic turns upon what distinguishes Rosa Luxemburg from Lenin, the German social-democratic direction of Lenin. Moreover, the *Critique of the Gotha Program* already raised the problem of the functioning of the Party. I think that when the existence of the Party and its various problems moved to the forefront, the question of will was totally abandoned. For if one follows the concept of the Leninist Party—and in fact it's not even Lenin who first imagined it, but we call it this because it was conceived around him—here's what the Party should be.

Firstly, it is an organization thanks to the existence of which the proletariat reaches class consciousness. In other words, via the Party, individual and subjective wills become a sort of collective will. But this collective will must, without fail, be monolithic, as though it were an individual will. The Party transforms the multiplicity of individual wills into a collective will. And through this transformation it constitutes a class as subject. In other words, it makes a class into a sort of individual subject. It's in this way that the very idea of the proletariat is made possible. "The proletariat exists because the Party exists". It is through the existence of the Party and by way of this existence that the proletariat can exist. The Party is consequently the consciousness of the proletariat and at the same time, for the proletariat taken as a unique individual subject, its condition of existence. Is this not the first reason it has not been possible to analyze the different levels of will at their true worth?

Another reason stems from the fact that the Party as an organization is hierarchically stratified. And it functioned well within this solidly hierarchized order—long before Leninist theory, German social democracy already worked this way—by excluding, by forbidding this or that thing. It was nothing other than an organization that excluded heretical elements and which, by operating in this way, sought to conflate the individual wills of the militants into a sort of monolithic will. This monolithic will was nothing other than the bureaucratic will of the leaders. Since things unfolded in this manner, this second reason resulted in the important problem of will never really being addressed. Put another way, the Party could always justify itself one way or another, as regards its activities, its decisions, and its role. Whatever the situation, the Party could invoke the theory of Marx as being the sole truth. Marx was the sole authority, and, because of this, it was considered that the activities of the Party had their rational basis in him. The multiple individual wills were consequently sucked up by the Party, and, in turn, the will of the Party disappeared behind the mask of a rational calculation consistent with theory passing for truth. Hence the different levels of will were bound to elude analysis. The problem of knowing how the individual wills in revolution and in struggle were articulated in relation to the different levels of will seems to me, too, to be a key issue, the responsibility for which falls to us. Indeed, today these multiple wills arebeginning to spring up in the gaps in the hegemony held by the traditional left. To be honest, this problem is not sufficiently highlighted in my works, and I barely mentioned it in The Will to Knowledge, in the form of a strategy from the perspective of state power. It might be that this theory of will, or the analysis of these heterogeneous levels, operates more efficiently in Japan than anywhere else. Perhaps there is something specific to the Japanese Communist Party, or some relation to Eastern philosophy. Anyway, in that regard, I'd like to talk about the other problem you broached, namely, the very somber and solitary tonality that the struggles necessarily assume. This aspect of struggle has scarcely been envisaged in Europe or in France. Or we can say, at least, that it has been envisaged too little. Why? I touched upon one of the reasons in my response to the last question. The first reason is the fact that the objective of the struggles is always obscured by the prophesy. Hence the solitary aspects too got concealed under the mask of prophesy. The second reason is the following. Since it was believed that the Party alone was the authentic owner of the struggle, and since this Party was a hierarchical organization capable of rational decision, those zones imbued with a somber madness, namely the dark side of human activity or the obscurely desolate zones—in spite of being the unavoidable lot of every struggle—had trouble emerging into broad daylight. Probably only works that are not theoretical, works that are literary, or perhaps Nietzsche, have spoken about it. It doesn't seem relevant here to insist on the difference between literature and philosophy, but what is certain is that on the level of theory we have not managed to do justice to this somber and solitary aspect of struggle.

For that very reason we must increase awareness of this inadequate aspect of theory. We will have to tear down the idea that philosophy is the only normative thought. The voices of an incalculable number of speaking subjects must resonate, and we must allow an innumerable experience to speak. The speaking subject shouldn't always be the same one. The normative words of philosophy should not be the only ones heard. We need to bring forth all sorts of experiences, lend our ear to aphasics, to the excluded, to the dying. Because we are on the outside; whereas they are the ones who confront the somber and solitary aspect of the struggles. I believe that the task of a practitioner of philosophy living in the West is to lend an ear to all these voices.

R. Yoshimoto: Listening to you, I have become aware, on a number of points, of ideas that up to now I have not read in your books. Many things have been made clear, it has been very instructive for me and for that I am very grateful.

There is just one point on which I'd like to express my opinion. It's when you mentioned Lenin's method. What did he do? How, at a later stage, were the Leninist Party and the Soviet Union transformed? What is the state of things today? Rather than tackle all of these problems, I'd like to limit myself to Lenin's ideas, and to say a few words about where I diverge from you.

This is a critique that arises naturally from the moment we tried to revive the theory of will: I reproach Lenin with having identified the will of the State and the organ of the State.

To the question "What is the State?" Lenin replied that it is the organ of class repression. In consequence the problem of knowing how to resist repression encompasses the whole question of the State. Now, historically, the State took over religion, philosophy, law, morality, but this whole problematic was swept aside. The only question asked is that of knowing how to conduct the struggle for class liberation against the organ of class repression. As a result, all the current and historical questions concerning the State remained unexplored.

On the other hand, in response to the question "What is the State?" our thinking was: as soon as one posits the power of the State, it's the manifestation of will. What I mean by this is that the State is not synonymous with government as the organ of class repression. The government is, in some sense, the body of the will of the State, but it is not the State's will itself. I think we need first of all to distinguish between the will of the State and the organ of the State. One could speak of a cult of class struggle: the end justifying the means, they completely set aside the problems of morality, of good and evil, and of religion; without going so far as to ignore these, they are granted only subsidiary or secondary importance. All because, probably, they identified from the outset the will of the State with the organ of the State, by referring immediately to class repression.

This is a critique that I have developed concerning the conception of the State in Lenin, at the level of ideas. Listening to you speak, I said to myself that at least on this point I had to express my opinion. As concerns the specific problems you are working on, there are many I would like to ask you about. In many areas, moreover, I thought I noted a certain number of shared topics that I'd also like to ask you about. But on the essential problems, the ones I am thinking about at the moment and that I'm having some difficulty elucidating, I think you have pretty much answered me.

Forgive me for having bothered you with difficult questions. I am infinitely grateful to you for your patience. I have already talked quite enough, and I would be happy if you would bring our interview to a close.

M. Foucault: I am very happy to have been able to listen to you and I thank you from the depth of my heart. Everything you have said will be very useful to me. For, on the one hand, thanks to your way of framing problems, you have perfectly indicated the limits of the work I have carried out to date and the places where it is still lacking, for want of clear ideas. And, notably, the problem that you bring up in terms of the theory of will is of particular interest to me, and I am convinced that it can serve as a pertinent point of departure for a whole series of problematics.

When I see even a simple résumé of your work and the list of your publications, I note that it often concerns the individual phantasm and the problem of the State. Moreover, as you just mentioned, you have devoted an essay to the collective will as a matrix in the formation of a State. For me, this is a fascinating problem. This year I am giving a course on the formation of the State in which I analyze, let's say, the basis of the means of establishing a State over a period running from the 16th century to the 18th century in the West, or rather the process over the course of which what we call state policy (*la raison d'état*) takes shape. But I have run up against a mysterious part that can't be resolved by any simple analysis of economic, institutional, or cultural relations. There is a sort of gigantic and irrepressible thirst that forces one to turn to the State. One could speak of a desire for the State. Or, to use the terms we have been using up to now, one could reformulate it as a will to State. In any case, it is clear that we can no longer avoid this type of thing.

Whenever the formation of a State is concerned, it is no longer a matter of figures such as the despot, or of its manipulation by men belonging to the upper caste. But one can only say that it has involved a kind of great love, an ungraspable will. As I was already fully aware of this, I had much to learn from what you told me today, and I am very curious to read your other works in which you discuss the State from the perspective of the theory of will.

I sincerely hope that your books will be translated into French or English. Alternatively, I would be happy, either in Tokyo, in Paris, or by correspondence to exchange ideas with you, since you seem to deal with the same themes. For to be able to listen to this sort of discourse is, for us Westerners, a precious and indispensable experience.

In particular, discussing a problem such as political experience in our era will not only prolong my life, but it will also be, I believe, an extremely enriching stimulus for future studies.

Translated by Peter Connor

NOTE

1 An allusion to the struggle against the construction of the new airport in Tokyo on the agricultural site of Narita.

8

MICHEL FOUCAULT AND ZEN

A Stay in a Zen Temple

"M. Foucault to zen: zendera taiza-ki" ("Michel Foucault et le zen: un séjour dans un temple zen"); an interview with C. Polak, in Umi, no. 197, August–September 1978, pp. 1–6.

Working on the history of Christian discipline, Foucault wished to better understand the practice of Zen and was invited to stay at the Seionji Temple in Uenohara in Yamanashi Prefecture, where Master Omori Sogen led the meditation room. An editor of the Buddhist review Shunjû recorded some of the interviews with the bonzes, which Christian Polak translated into French.

Dits et écrits III, no. 236

M. Foucault: I don't know if I am capable of correctly following the rigorous rules of the Zen temple, but I'll do my best. I am very interested in the philosophy of Buddhism. But that's not the reason I have come this time. What most interests me is life itself at the temple, specifically

DOI: 10.4324/9781003303763-10

the practice of Zen, the training and the rules. For I think that a totally different mentality from ours takes shape through the practice and training at a Zen temple. Just now, you told us that this is a living temple that differs from traditional temples. Do you have different rules from other temples?

A Monk: I meant that this temple is not representative of Zen culture. In this sense, this temple is perhaps not entirely satisfactory. There is an expression that says "Zen represents man". We have a number of monks here who ardently pursue Zen in itself. This is what living Zen means.

M. Foucault: Regarding my memories of my first stay in Japan, I have rather a feeling of regret at having seen nothing and understood nothing. That certainly doesn't mean I wasn't shown anything. But during and even after I traveled around in order to observe many things, I felt I hadn't grasped anything. For me, from the point of view of the technology, the lifestyle, the appearance of the social structure, as a country Japan is extremely close to the Western world. Yet at the same time the inhabitants of this country seem to me on every level much more mysterious than those of the other countries of the world. What impressed me was this mix of proximity and distance. And I wasn't able to get any clearer impression than that.

A Monk: I was told that almost all of your works are translated into Japanese. Do you think your ideas are well understood?

M. Foucault: I have no way of knowing how people interpret the work I have carried out. It is always a great surprise to me that my work is translated abroad and even that my work is read in France. Frankly, I hope my work interests ten or a hundred people. And if it turns out to be a larger number, I am always a bit surprised. In my view it's because my name, Foucault, is easy to pronounce in Japanese, much easier for example than Heidegger. That's a joke, of course. I think that someone who writes has no right to demand to be understood as he wanted to be when he wrote. In other words, from the moment he writes he is no longer the owner of what he says, except from a juridical perspective. Obviously if someone critiques you and proves you wrong while misinterpreting your arguments, you can insist on what it was you were trying to express. But besides cases such as that, I think that the freedom of the reader should absolutely be respected. Discourse is a reality than can be infinitely transformed. Hence the one who writes does not have the right to give orders with respect to the use of his writings.

I don't consider what I write to be an oeuvre in the original and classical sense of this word. I write things that seem usable. In sum, usable in a different sense, by different people, in different countries in certain cases. So if I analyze something like madness or power and it is useful for something, that's enough. That's the reason I write. If someone uses what I write differently, it's not unpleasant for me, and even if it's used in another context for something else, I am quite content. In this sense I don't think that I am the author of the work and that the thought and the intention of the author have to be respected.

A Monk: Is your interest in Japan deep or superficial?

M. Foucault: To be honest I am not constantly interested in Japan. What interests me is the Western history of rationality and its limit. In this respect Japan raises a problem we cannot escape, and is an illustration of this problem. For Japan is an enigma, very difficult to decipher. This does not mean that it is what stands opposed to Western rationality. In reality, everywhere else Western rationality builds colonies, whereas in Japan it is far from building one, on the contrary, rather, it is colonized by Japan.

A Monk: I was told that you are interested in mysticism. In your view, do mysticism and esoterism mean the same thing?

M. Foucault: No.

A Monk: Do you think that Zen is a Japanese mysticism?

M. Foucault: As you know, Zen was born in India, developed in China, and arrived in Japan in the 13th century. So I don't think it is really

Japanese. Rinzai is a Zen monk I like a lot and he is not Japanese.[1] He is neither a translator of the sutras nor a founder of Chinese Zen, but I consider him a great philosopher of Zen. He is from the 9th century, right? I read the French version by Professor Demiéville, who is an excellent French specialist of Buddhism.

A Monk: It seems that most Japanese specialists think that Buddhism originated in China rather than India.

M. Foucault: The idea that Zen originated in India is perhaps a bit mythological. It is probably to link Zen to the Buddha himself. Zen in India isn't very important. Indeed, it evolved considerably in China in the 7th century and in Japan in the 13th century, did it not?

A Monk: What do you think about the relation between Zen and mysticism?

M. Foucault: I think that Zen is totally different from Christian mysticism. But I think that Zen is a mysticism. That said, I don't know enough about Zen to be able to defend this belief. We could say in any case that it has almost nothing in common with Christian mysticism, whose tradition goes back to Saint Bernard, Saint Theresa of Avila, Saint John of the Cross. It's completely different. When I say mysticism, I am using the term in the Christian sense. What is very impressive about Christian spirituality and its technique is that it is always seeking greater individualization. It tries to grasp what there is deep in the soul of the individual. "Tell me who you are"—that's the spirituality of Christianity. As for Zen, it seems that on the contrary all the techniques linked to spirituality tend to attenuate the individual. Zen and Christian mysticism are two things one can't compare, whereas the techniques of Christian spirituality and of Zen are comparable. And here a great contrast exists. In Christian mysticism, even when it preaches the union of God and the individual, something individual remains. Because it is a matter of the relations of love between God and the individual. One loves, and the other is loved. In short, Christian mysticism seeks individualization.

ON ZEN MEDITATION

M. Foucault: With so little experience, I can't say anything very precise. In spite of that, if I was able to feel something through the posture of the body in Zen meditation, that is to say the correct position of the body, it is new relationships that can exist between the mind and the body and, in addition, new relationships between the body and the external world. We don't have much time. I'd like to ask you just one question. It's about the universality of Zen. Is it possible to separate the practice of Zen from the totality of the religion and from the practice of Buddhism?

Omori: Zen is born from Buddhism. There are therefore close ties between Zen and Buddhism. However, Zen does not necessarily require the form of Zen. One can even abandon the name "Zen". Zen is much more free.

You just said that you felt new relationships between the mind and the body and between the body and the external world. I find you admirable to have felt this with so little experience of Zen. Don't you agree that these are universal experiences—to feel that the body and the mind come together and that the mind and the external world come together? This goes to show that Zen has an international and universal character. Zen is small if you think it is only a part of Buddhism, but we do not look at it as a part of Buddhism. If your experience allowed you to understand Zen in this sense, I think you would be convinced of the universality of Zen.

A Monk: I am very happy to welcome to my little Japanese town, Uenohara, a great philosopher such as you.

M. Foucault: I am not a great philosopher, as you say. I am the one who is happy to participate in this ceremony.[2] I was not expecting to be able to attend such an event.

A Monk: Regarding the crisis of Western thought that is dominating Europe right now, do you think that Eastern thought might contribute to a reconsideration of Western thought? That is to say, do you think that Eastern thought might in some way allow Western thought to find a new way?

M. Foucault: Reexamination of these subjects is being carried out by various means, through psychoanalysis, anthropology, and the analysis of history. And I do think that the reexaminations could be furthered by confronting Western thought with Eastern thought.

Indeed, European thought is at a turning point. This turning point, on the historical level, is nothing other than the end of imperialism. The crisis of Western thought is identical to the end of imperialism. This crisis has not produced any supreme philosopher who excels in signifying the crisis itself. For Western thought in crisis expresses itself through discourses that can be very interesting but are neither specific nor extraordinary. There is no philosopher who marks this epoch. For it is the end of the era of Western philosophy. Thus, if a philosophy of the future exists, it must be born outside of Europe or it must be born of encounters and reverberations between Europe and non-Europe.

A Monk: What do you think of the spread of Western thought and of its universality?

M. Foucault: Europe is located in a specific region of the world and in a specific epoch. That said, it has the peculiarity of having created a universal category that characterizes the modern world. Europe is the birthplace of universality. In this sense, the crisis of European thought draws the attention of everybody and concerns everybody. It's a crisis that influences the different ways of thinking in all countries of the world, as well as the general thinking of the world. For example, Marxism was born in a specific epoch in a specific region, it was founded by a Jew through contact with a handful of workers. It became not only an ideological form but a world view, a social organization. Marxism lays claim to universality, and moreover, as you know, in spite of a bit of resistance, it is reflected worldwide.

Now, Marxism is currently indisputably in a crisis. The crisis of Western thought, the crisis of the Western concept that is revolution, the crisis of the Western concepts that are man and society. It's a crisis that concerns the whole world and that concerns the Soviet Union as much as it does Brazil, Czechoslovakia, Cuba, etc.

A Monk: On the topic of Marxism, what do you think about its future and what do think of Eurocommunism?

M. Foucault: In my view, one of the important things in what is being called the crisis of Marxism is the fact that Marxism is no longer useful as the theoretical guarantee of the Communist Party. The Communist Party is no longer Marxist. This is also the case in the Soviet Union, in countries with a popular democracy, in France, and in Cuba.

As regards Eurocommunism, the important question today is not about its future, but about the idea and theme of revolution. Since 1789, Europe has changed in function of the idea of revolution. European history has been dominated by this idea. It is precisely this idea which is in the process of disappearing today.

A Monk: Here is my last question. In your view, what should the Japan of the future be?

M. Foucault: My answer is simple. I think that the role of intellectuals, in truth, absolutely doesn't consist in playing at being prophets or legislators. For 2000 years, philosophers have always talked about what should be done. But that always translated into a tragic end. What is important is that philosophers talk about what is happening today, not what might happen.

[…]

M. Foucault: I have already visited several Zen temples. I had the impression they were closed, cold, or cut off from the outer world. But yours has given me a very clear impression of a temple that is open and integrated into its environment.

I thank you for having given me this experience of Zen, which will be very precious to me. But it is a modest experience. I hope to be able to return in a year or two to acquire more experience.

Translated by Peter Connor

NOTES

1 Rinzai (Linji), died in 867 CE. One of the great Zen Masters of the Tang dynasty.

2 A memorial service for children who die before birth (*mizuko kuyo*).

FOUCAULT IN JAPAN

An Interview with Shiguéhiko Hasumi

Shiguéhiko Hasumi, a distinguished film and literary critic and Professor Emeritus and former President of the University of Tokyo, was one of the key figures who helped introduce Foucault to the Japanese public. His interview with Foucault, conducted in Paris in October 1977, opens The Japan Lectures.

But the relations between the two go back much earlier. In 1970, Foucault had made an earlier trip to Japan and, shortly after, Hasumi published an interview with him, in which, as later in 1977, the focus was on Foucault's relations with Marx and Marxism; he also attended a lecture on Manet that Foucault gave in Japan, which would give him pause. Early on, Hasumi had studied at the University of Tokyo with Maurice Pinguet, a classmate of Foucault, specializing in Japan, with whom Foucault would have sustained relations.[1] Hasumi later studied at the Sorbonne in the '60s, where he wrote his dissertation on Flaubert. When Hasumi started teaching at the University of Tokyo, he and Pinguet became colleagues and developed a friendly relationship, eventually living in close proximity, near central Tokyo.

Foucault's second trip to Japan in 1978 came at a different moment in his own work and its translation and discussion in Japan. In his interview with Hasumi in Paris in 1977, he would set out the larger problem he hoped to develop during this trip; and Hasumi would participate in various ways in the reception and discussion of the lectures

DOI: 10.4324/9781003303763-11

and related activities during his visit. Along with Moriaki Watanabe, Hasumi belongs to a first generation who helped introduce Foucault's work to Japan, functioning as "interceders" in a zone in-between the two countries and related publics and academic institutions. Not themselves students of academic philosophy, they instead exemplify the sort of "non-philosopher" of which philosophy has need, and to whom it is addressed, perhaps now as much as ever, in many different places throughout the world. Following his study with Pinguet, Hasumi maintained a keen sense of the role a great university might play in providing for, and in some cases countering the suppression of, this sort of free, open, unscripted cross-cultural discussion; and along with Watanabe, he helped encourage new publishing and research ventures in "critical theory". In 1991, Hasumi organized an international symposium on Foucault's work in Tokyo entitled "Michel Foucault's Century". His presentation of its title theme would be translated into French in 1994, just before the publication of Dits et écrits.[2] Watanabe and Hasumi thus played a different role, going back much earlier, than did Christian Polak and Thierry de Beaucé at the French Embassy, who organized Foucault's visit, later helping with the selection and publication of the lectures in Dits et écrits; Polak and Beaucé kept, as well, additional materials (one translated by Hasumi) now at IMEC (Institut Mémoires de l'édition contemporaine), involving in particular an extended interaction with Masao Maruyama and a long letter from Ryumei Yoshimoto, which shed light on Foucault's larger political engagement at the time and the ways it figures in The Japan Lectures.[3]

A participant, sometimes a witness, with his own ongoing role as a cinema and literary critic and a university professor, Hasumi thus had a peculiar vantage point on this long-forgotten moment in Foucault's itinerary, which The Japan Lectures now serve to re-open. I was therefore delighted that he was willing to look back at it in the context of this new publication in English, this time as interviewee. But I was not prepared for the remarkable manner in which he would bring to his detailed responses in this retrospective interview the same sort of independence of spirit and curiosity he displayed at the time. The interview, conducted in Tokyo and New York in August 2022, was, at his suggestion, conducted in English and Japanese (translated by Ryan Cook and arranged by Yuma Terada and Ryosuke Saegusa of CTB Inc.); it thus recaptures something of the "translinguistic" character of the original Lectures themselves and the circumstances and processes through which they came to be translated in many languages and places. The resulting suggestive complexity of his response raises many questions that go beyond the actual interview.

Foucault made two trips to Japan, part of an ongoing relation, connected in part with his friendship with Maurice Pinguet, a fellow "Normalien", who went on to live and work in Japan. Before turning to Foucault's lectures in 1978, I'd like to ask a few questions about this earlier phase in his relations with Japan.

1. *You conducted a remarkable earlier interview with Foucault shortly after his first trip to Japan, published in 1973. How did that come about?*

You are referring, more precisely, to something published in the March 1973 issue of the Japanese literary magazine Umi, based on an interview I had conducted with Foucault at his home at 289 Rue de Vaugirard in the XVe arrondissement of Paris on September 27, 1972, shortly before my return to Japan from my second extended stay in France from 1971 to 1972. I remember being quite surprised, and also nervous, when Foucault quickly responded in the affirmative to my written request for an interview. At the time, I was religiously attending his weekly lectures at the Collège de France, and I had of course read Les Mots et les choses, but also L'Archéologie du savoir—both closely and with a great deal of interest.

If pressed to say in what way the country of Japan might have brought about a change in the Foucault of 1970, I think he probably began to place a certain degree of confidence in the activities of what can be called Japan's intellectual publications, periodicals dedicated to literature and contemporary thought. This is something probably not unrelated to the very high quality of the dialogue that Tōru Shimizu and Moriaki Watanabe held with Foucault, "Folie, littérature, société", which was the only interview conducted at the time of Foucault's first stay in Japan in 1970.

The very fact that, before returning to France, Foucault entrusted his highly significant text "Réponse à Jacques Derrida" to Mikitaka Nakano, the lead editor of the quarterly journal *Paideia*, is quite symbolic in this respect. At the time, this had not yet been published even in France. I distinctly remember the excitement I felt when I was unexpectedly shown this manuscript from him. Foucault's intellectual activity was basically unknown among Japanese intellectuals in 1970, but within the space of ten years he would become a mega-celebrity. Several people in the publishing world played significant roles in establishing his reputation in Japan as a leading intellectual figure, starting with the aforementioned Mikitaka Nakano (now deceased), and including the late Akira (Ken) Yasuhara, editor of the literary magazine *Umi*, and the late Yoshihiko Hanawa, who would eventually take over as editor of the same publication (and who attended the University of Tokyo as a student alongside his close friend Kenzaburō Ōe).

2. *What were your relations with Maurice Pinguet? In what ways do you see him as influencing Foucault's views about or his relations with Japan?*

I will take this opportunity to talk a little about Maurice Pinguet since I knew him. Following his arrival in Japan in 1958, I first encountered Maurice Pinguet as his student. We later became colleagues and developed a friendly relationship. After 1970, we both lived near Higashi-Matsubara train station on the Inokashira line in Setagaya, a part of the city that basically neighbors central Tokyo. We would visit each other at our respective homes and had dinner together on more than a few occasions up until his later years. When he was writing *Mort volontaire au Japon*, we had discussions and I would answer his various questions, meeting him at cafes and sometimes talking on the phone. However, I never once talked with him about Foucault. As a result, and pertaining to your question, I unfortunately have no knowledge of where Pinguet took Foucault, who he introduced him to, or what he described to him about Japan, during his first visit. Even if I did have some kind of pertinent knowledge, I would not have a basis for judging whether this involved "influence" on Foucault by Maurice Pinguet. For one thing, I am generally quite skeptical about the idea of personal "influence" among individuals, however close they may be as intellectuals. I believe that influence in the true sense does not come from a particular person, but from the impersonal form of the written word—in other words, from writing where the question of the person behind it does not have much significance, whether the writing takes the form of fiction, criticism, or a research paper.

Maurice Pinguet came to Japan in 1958 as a foreign lecturer at the University of Tokyo just as I was entering the graduate school of Humanities there. The biggest lesson that I took from him was the attitude with which he approached the university as an institution, an attitude of thorough "disdain". His perspective was informed by the French higher education system at the time. There is no doubt that as a product of the École Normale Supérieure (rue d'Ulm), Pinguet was deeply suspicious of the Sorbonne (which was the home of literature and the humanities within the University of Paris system at the time). In this respect, my own life as a graduate student started, quite literally, with Maurice Pinguet's feelings of contempt for the university. Before his courses had started, I heard that this new French instructor was a specialist in the work of André Saurès and I rushed to the library to read through some of Suarès's writings. I clearly recall as if it were yesterday how impossible it was for me to understand what I read as a young Japanese man, just 21 years old. Pinguet's approach with us graduate students was to ignore our French speaking and listening ability completely, instead making someone read a book and present on it in French each time we met. None of us had studied in France at that point and our pronunciation was mostly quite clumsy. After the presentations, Pinguet would then comment critically. I presented on Jean-Pierre Richard's *Littérature et sensation*, and a good friend presented on Lucien Goldmann's *Dieu caché*. After his critiques of our presentations, Pinguet would suddenly change his tone and advise us that if we were to study in the University of Paris system on a French government scholarship, it would be best to avoid mentioning the names Richard and Goldmann in front of the faculty there.

At first, I did not understand the significance of this, but the literature classes I later experienced first-hand at the University of Paris in the early 1960s turned out to be old-fashioned. There were professors who would go on for an entire hour criticizing Jean-Paul Sartre on Baudelaire, for example, while entirely ignoring the context in which Sartre had written that study. Courses in literary studies in that moment at the University of Paris, which is to say the Sorbonne, were reactionary and dull. A certain professor who was a committee member for my University of Paris dissertation on Flaubert's *Madame Bovary* (*Méthode pscyhologique de Flaubert d'après* Madame Bovary) strongly critiqued me for citing a questionable critic like Jean-Pierre Richard in a doctoral thesis. My advisor, Professor Robert Ricatte, was an exception to this tendency at the University of Paris. He was open-minded and also had a strong interest in what were then new tendencies in literary research. He responded with sharp criticism to the other committee member's reactionary statements. Watching these two professors argue with each other as if I were not even in the room, despite the fact that I was the one defending the thesis, made me understand concretely for the first time what Pinguet had earlier said to us young Japanese students. Fortunately, Professor Ricatte was running a literature seminar at the École Normale Supérieure, to which he would invite people like Jean-Pierre Richard, but also Jean Starovinski and Jean Rousset. This was refreshing and motivating to me and other young students. Needless to say, this also gave me a deep understanding of the mistrust Maurice Pinguet had displayed in front of his young Japanese students with respect to the French university system of the time.

Later, I would be blessed with two occasions to disdain the University of Tokyo in turn. These experiences were related to the visits of Roland Barthes and Michel Foucault, respectively, both of whom Pinguet had invited to Japan. When Barthes first came to Japan in 1966, I went with Pinguet to greet him at the old Haneda Airport in my role as an assistant in the University of Tokyo Faculty of Letters, one of the institutions that was hosting him. Encountering an exhausted Barthes as he appeared at the edge of a dim passageway in this antiquated airport left a deep impression. I had been a staunch Barthes advocate in the

Barthes–Picard debate that had taken place shortly before my departure from Paris and volunteered to serve as interpreter when he was slated to lecture at the University of Tokyo. Shortly before the event, a professor who had glanced at his CV observed in a faculty meeting that Barthes was not on the faculty at the University of Paris and seemed not even to have written a doctoral dissertation. The professor argued that he was not qualified to give a public address at the University of Tokyo, and the prospect loomed that his lecture might be canceled. Barthes was, in fact, not a University of Paris faculty member at the time. His position was Directeur d'Études at the École des Hautes Études en Sciences Sociales (EHESS), an institution unconnected to the University of Paris. The idea of canceling a lecture by Barthes, who was at the heights of illustriousness in France at the time, was so preposterous to me that I deliberately mistranslated his French CV into Japanese to read "Professor at the Institut des Hautes Études en Sciences Sociales, University of Paris" and resubmitted it to the deans, and the event ultimately went forward. In my role as an assistant, I had deliberately misrepresented Barthes's CV, committing a clearly criminal act. It goes without saying that I felt deep "contempt" for the University of Tokyo in this moment.

I was also blessed with an opportunity to feel clear "contempt" for the University of Tokyo in relation to Foucault. In the late 1960s I was working at a different university, and so I only learned indirectly, through rumors, about things happening internally at the University of Tokyo. According to what I had heard, there had been a proposal to invite Michel Foucault there as successor to Maurice Pinguet who, during one of my stays in France, had stepped down from his lecturer position in order to become the director of the Institut Franco-Japonais. But at the time, foreign nationals were not eligible for the title of Professor at the University of Tokyo, and so Foucault could only be made a lecturer, not a professor. Foucault already had the rank of Professor at the University of Clermont-Ferrand and should have been offered a commensurate salary, but the University of Tokyo maintained that it could only bring him on as a lecturer, a position that came with a salary that could hardly be called generous. This, of course, made me feel deep "contempt".

I leave it to you to determine how to assess the ironic circumstances in which someone who twice experienced heartfelt "contempt" for the University of Tokyo in relation to Maurice Pinguet later became President of the same university after Pinguet's death.

3. *Foucault also gave a lecture at the time entitled* Revenir à l'histoire *(Returning to History) in which he talks about challenging monolithic historical narratives in favor of something more like "multiple temporalities". How do you see this lecture among those he gave at the time?*

Foucault's lecture "Revenir à l'histoire", which took place on October 9, 1970, at Keio University in Tokyo was published two years later in *Paideia*, and I myself was in the audience when he gave it. Because this was over half a century ago I have only a vague memory of it, but I confess in all honesty that it did not strike me as a particularly impressive lecture for Foucault. I felt that he was too unguarded, too generous toward various tendencies of the structuralism that was in fashion in France in the 1960s. Or looking back now, perhaps I felt that this lecture, given in 1970, too conspicuously reflected the intellectual exaltation of "1960s France", or that it lacked sufficient remove from the frenzy of "68". These impressions remained even after I read the text of the lecture published in the second volume of *Dits et écrits*. I can to a certain extent understand how Foucault was determined to rescue a series of efforts that could be classified as structuralist from "une critique d'inspiration phénoménologique ou existentielle" (*Dits et écrits*, p. 270), something not unrelated to the language he used to describe the critics of *Les Mots et les choses* and *L'Archéologie du savoir* when he dismissed them during my interview with him in 1972 as "marxistes empiriques et mous" (*Dits et écrits*, p. 406), and on another occasion as "marxistes sommaires" (*Dits et écrits*, p. 271). But it is hard not to detect a certain degree of overstatement, or an intentional deflection, in his assertions that all his work at its starting point, whether "éthnographique" or "linguistique" or "littéraire", belonged to "des tentatives pour se donner l'instrument d'une analyse historique" (ibid.). He also writes that, "Barthes, en introduisant cette notion d'écriture, a voulu fonder une nouvelle possibilité d'histoire littéraire" (*Dits et écrits II*, p, 270), but is this actually correct? It is hard to think of this as anything but a very convenient point of view for Foucault. It seems to me that what was important for Barthes was above all to "cease to be himself" through writing.

For the reasons stated above, I do not believe that Foucault's 1970 trip to Japan had any particular influence on his thinking about history. I also do not think that his lecture in Japan, "Revenir à l'histoire", was what you call "another turning point" in his thinking about history. I say this because I think he was consistent in his attachment to "history" from the time of his 1963 *Naissance de la clinique: une archéologie du regard médical*. He did certainly adopt the position of "a rejection of monolithic periods", as you put it, but I think this is something characteristic of Foucault that can also be observed in his writings from before the time of this lecture. Foucault did use the language "une histoire dite 'sérielle'" (*Dits et écrits II*, p. 276) numerous times in his lecture, but unfortunately, I am not aware of whether he subsequently continued to use the modifier "sérielle" with any frequency. On this point, I would be interested in knowing your thoughts as a Foucault expert.

Please indulge me for a brief word about "Réponse à Derrida", which was published in Japan around the same time as Foucault's Japan lecture "Revenir à l'histoire". This is among the most remarkable of texts on Derrida, and to the extent that its content is what you have in mind when you speak of "a rejection of textualism", this description even seems a bit narrow as a summary characterization given how substantive that text is. I would like to point out, incidentally, that there is an error in the Romanization of the Japanese in the explanatory commentary that appears at the front of this text in *Dits et écrits*. My edition reads "Derrida he no kairo" (*Dits et écrits II*, p. 281), but the Japanese word for "réponse" is not *kairo*. The correct word is *kaitō*. To read the text itself is to encounter such a wonderful *textualization* of Foucault's language that calling its content "a rejection of textualism" seems too narrow. The text is organized in such a way that it seems like an exemplar, a demonstration of how properly to have a debate. I am very attached to this response, in particular because, as already mentioned, I was one of the first people in the world to lay eyes on the typed manuscript.

4. *A few years later, Roland Barthes joined a notorious trip of French intellectuals to Beijing, publishing his reactions in "Alors, la Chine?". How do you see this intervention, and what kinds of reactions were there to it in Japan at the time?*

The real trouble with Barthes's "Alors, la Chine?" lies in the fact that there was no Maurice Pinguet, no longtime friend of Barthes, in China. It is easy to imagine that Sollers and Kristeva, whose relationship with Barthes was probably a strictly intellectual one, were not in a position to play this kind of role. It is also easy to imagine, given Barthes's personality, that he would not have been especially fond of traveling in a group. As a result, the kind of view he attempted to form of China was likely quite different from the view he formed of his surroundings during his trip to Japan with Pinguet as his guide. It is even possible that Barthes saw nothing in China—with the exception of his famously having tasted the "fadeur du thé vert" and of his escapist reading of *Bouvard et Pécuchet*.

As for the reaction among intellectuals in Japan to this short essay, I cannot offer any generalizations. It is hard to imagine that there were many who cited it, whether sympathetically or critically, upon its initial publication. If there is anything I can say in connection with *Empire des signes*, it is probably that I personally have never felt a strong attraction to this piece of writing. But I have also never opposed recognizing it as a "happy" text. There are two "happy" texts by Barthes from around this time, which is to say texts written "dans une sorte d'état euphorique": *Michelet par lui-même* and *Empire des signes*. I vividly recall how happy Barthes himself was when I conveyed this impression to him ("Pour la libération d'une pensée pluraliste", Roland Barthes, *Œuvres complètes*, Tome II, p. 1999).

The later response of European intellectuals to the so-called "Cultural Revolution" in China, a tendency that the Tiananmen Square Incident eventually put to rest around ten years after Foucault's second visit to Japan, was something that I cannot help but see as a kind of reverse "Orientalism". This tendency, which for convenience we can say was represented by Jean-Luc Godard's film *Le Vent d'est*, forms a contrast with the press conference in Japan of February 28, 1967, jointly organized by the writers Yasunari Kawabata, Jun Ishikawa, Kōbō Abe, and Yukio Mishima in protest at the Cultural Revolution in China. It would be wrong to look at the presence of Yukio Mishima here and draw the conclusion that this was a group manifesto by so-called right-wing authors. Jun Ishikawa and Kōbō Abe were very free writers who went about their creative work in contexts thoroughly unrelated to such kinds of political tendencies. Perhaps they were imagining the many acts of folly committed in China by Japanese militarists during the 1930s and saw dangerous indications of similar things in the China of the Cultural Revolution era.

I will add that postwar Japan did not restore diplomatic relations with China until 1970. Zhou Enlai, who had studied abroad in Japan, played a leading role in this process, and was a very important figure during this period, having also lived through the Cultural Revolution without being purged. It is a tragic aspect of China today that perhaps no one like Zhou Enlai is anywhere to be found.

Let's turn now to Foucault's second trip to Japan in 1978, from which the Japan Lectures are taken. I'd like first to ask some questions about the general context and subsequent effects there.

5. *In 2011, in an essay entitled "Vent d'Ouest", Hidetaka Ishida (Director of the Japanese translation of Dits et écrits) suggests that together with Moriaki Watanabe, you helped stimulate a new interest and related research in "theory" or "contemporary thought" (gendai shiso), which would later be taken up by several generations in the discussion and translation of Foucault. You and Watanabe were both "non-philosophers", who played a role in the University of Tokyo, each working in other areas of interest. I gather your own came in part through cinema?*

Despite Hidetaka Ishida's testimony to the contrary, I myself have not translated any full text by Foucault. Moriaki Watanabe was also not very early in introducing Foucault, since his translation of La volonté de savoir (Histoire de la sexualité, vol. 1) was only published in 1986. What Ishida probably meant to say in this context is that our references to Foucault, both direct and indirect, had a certain effect of stimulation among young people who encountered them, especially since they came from non-philosophers.

Forgive me for speaking honestly, but I cannot help feeling a strong resistance to the idea of lumping our pioneering allusions to Foucault together with "*gendai shisō*" ("contemporary thought"). "*Shisō*/thought" is premised on the baseless conviction that, when faced with a text, it is possible, through meticulous application of suitable logic and description, to arrive at the "truth" of the thinking (*shikō*)[4] that is in the process of being expressed. My position is that prose discourse of all kinds, whether novelistic or theoretical, is essentially fiction at its limits, that discourse is something that conceals "truth", or intercepts thinking as it moves toward it, something that sometimes can even suddenly expunge it from view. This is why I was drawn to Foucault's *Les mots et les choses*, because I saw that its language was everywhere charged with invitations into this kind of fiction.

As for what enticed me personally toward cinema, the answer is quite simply the rich filmgoing experience of my middle school years. The unanticipated emergence of "*gendai shisō*/contemporary thought" bore no relation whatsoever. In fact, I was already publishing film commentaries by the time I was an undergraduate, commentaries in commercial magazines on great films like *Elena et les hommes* (Jean Renoir, 1956), *Un condamné à mort s'est échappé* (Robert Bresson, 1956), and *The Hustler* (Robert Rossen, 1961). I was also deeply moved by *Ride the High Country* (aka *Guns in the Afternoon*, Sam Peckinpah, 1961), which I saw in 1962 right before I left Japan to attend the University of Paris. I felt dazzled by the newness of this film, which was different from both the classical Western as it had existed to that point and the postwar Western as represented by Anthony Mann. During the monthlong voyage by ship from Yokohama to Marseilles, I had the feeling that where I really belonged was on the west coast of the United States where this new film director Peckinpah lived, and I spent my days worrying that I was probably heading toward the wrong destination.

In 1969, following my return from France, I began teaching a film seminar at a certain private university in Tokyo, a year before I started my faculty position at the University of Tokyo. One of my students from that time was Kiyoshi Kurosawa, the director of *Wife of a Spy* (*Supai no tsuma*, 2020), which won the Leone d'Argento prize at the 77th Venice

International Film Festival in 2020. From this I think you can understand how removed my activities around film have been from "*gendai shisō*/contemporary thought"—not only removed, but existing in a whole different sphere.

For the abovementioned reasons, I am not in a position to testify as to whether Foucault contributed to the establishment of any kind of new "theory" in Japan. For Foucault, lecturing at a university in a small island country in the Far East must certainly have been something not quite the same as lecturing at universities located on the west coast of the United States. I think it is likely that people in Japan were strongly conscious of their own "otherness". But I cannot offer any detailed explanation of how or whether this relates to what you're referring to as "critical translation theory".

6. *In November 1991, you organized an international symposium in Tokyo entitled "Foucault's Century", contributing a striking lecture entitled "Foucault and the 19th Century", translated into French in 1994. One senses that you had some misgivings about the gross categories of "modernity" and "postmodernity" and Foucault's supposed role in them?*

A detail in Foucault's *Les mots et les choses* had strangely enticed me—as I have stated elsewhere in my talk "Foucault et le XIXe siècle" (*Magazine littéraire*, no. 325, 1994), which I presented at a 1991 University of Tokyo international symposium on Foucault's Century. It has to do with the way that Foucault, despite everywhere using the term *classique* without hesitation, insistently avoided use of the term, or qualifier, *moderne* in key parts of his writings, as, for example, where he writes in *Les mots et les choses*, "*Le seuil du classisme à la modernité (mais peu importent les mots eux-mêmes—disons de notre préhistoire à ce qui nous est encore contemporain)...*" (p. 315). This is also clear from the point in the same text where he purposely writes "*l'ordre sur le fond duquel nous pensons*" (p. 13) to refer to what any reader will accurately understand as "*l'épistème moderne*".

This hesitation, or self-restraint, around the word *moderne* is less a matter of attention to style than an expression of the basic position from which he confronts history. Perhaps he also worried that using the word *moderne* in writing to describe the world in which we live, much as people do quite naturally in speech by custom, would cause his understanding of history to lose meaning. I find Foucault's primitive hesitation around use of the word *moderne* tremendously beautiful. The beauty of this "knowing nothing" (*michi*)[5] brings to *Les mots et les chose* the power of fiction. I also think, even now, that viewed from this Foucauldian perspective, and also from my own quite personal perspective, the dualism of Modernity and Postmodernity that at a certain point caused quite a sensation in universities in the West, as well as in the Japanese mass media, was a mistaken way of posing the problem.

7. *How did the interview you conducted with Foucault in December of 1997, in anticipation of his trip to Japan, come about?*

Foucault's second visit to Japan in 1978 had originally been planned for the fall of 1977 but was for some reason deferred until the spring of the next year. At the beginning of the interview I conducted with him ("Pouvoir et savoir": interview with S. Hasumi recorded in Paris, October 13, 1977, *Umi*, December 1977), he explains apologetically that the cancelation was not his fault, so perhaps there was some administrative reason. The interview itself was something improvised, having come about by chance. At the time I was spending two or three weeks of every fall in Paris collecting materials for a book I was writing on Maxime Du Camp. I would confine myself from morning to night in the rare book department, which was then housed in the old Bibliothèque Nationale building on Rue de Richelieu. Foucault himself showed up there almost every day, but he gave off an air of unapproachability as he pored silently over his materials, one that severely discouraged untoward attempts at engagement. Trying to talk to him seemed utterly impossible.

One day I received a sudden phone call at my hotel from Yoshihiko Hanawa, the lead editor of *Umi*, who at the time was occasionally in Paris, having been a *stagaire* in the editorial section at *Le Nouvel Observateur* several years earlier. He informed me that Foucault's visit to Japan had been called off for that year but would apparently be happening later.

In preparation for what would probably be his upcoming visit, he asked if I would conduct an interview. At that point, I was not a very close reader of Foucault, having only read *Surveiller et punir* (1975) among his books, and having not yet looked at the already published first volume of his announced four-volume *Histoire de la sexualité*. I immediately went out and bought a copy of *La volonté de savoir* (1976) and crammed overnight in preparation, somehow following the sequence of facts but not without feeling a kind of misgiving. I somehow made it through but had no confidence whatsoever in the results of my preparations.

The interview took place at Foucault's apartment on Rue de Vaugirard, as in 1972, but when we entered, numerous people were bustling around, so much so that I thought we had perhaps mistaken the date. Foucault came out and greeted Hanawa and me, and explained that he had forgotten about an important meeting that was taking place at his home that day. He apologized and suggested moving to another space for the interview. He looked for a key and then we took the elevator to the second floor, then changed to another elevator from which he brought us to a small space like a *chambre de bonne*. Foucault was participating in various social movements at the time, and it seems that their meetings were taking place at his apartment.

He said we would not be bothered by telephones there and could go about our work in calm, then let out a flamboyant, animalistic laugh, stretched out on the floor, and proceeded very carefully to answer our questions. His demeanor was like that of a wise monkey on a plane far above that of human intellect, and when the interview was published in the December issue of the literary magazine *Umi*, I accompanied it with an explanatory text entitled "Provocations of a Wise Monkey" (*Sōmei na saru no chōhatsu*). Claude Mauriac supposedly said somewhere that Foucault's wild laugh recalled *les oiseaux de proie*, but to my ear, as someone from Asia, it reminded me of the laughter of monkeys, animals that are sometimes regarded as "wise". Note that the second half of the interview described here includes Foucault's responses to questions from Hanawa.

8. *What then was your own role in the various lectures and interventions during Foucault's trip?*

For some reason, my recollection of Foucault's 1978 visit to Japan has faded and I basically have no memories of that occasion. I must have attended his April 20, 1978, lecture "*Sexualité et pouvoir*" (*Dits et écrits III*, p. 552) which took place at the University of Tokyo's Komaba campus with Moriaki Watanabe as moderator, but I am now unable to remember exactly where or at what time the event was held or to call forth any visual memories. The transcript of the lecture in *Dits et Écrits* indicates that I asked a fairly long question, so I was clearly there, but the whole thing has become hazy, and I cannot recall a single detail. It would be possible to clarify things like the exact location and time from the documentation, but my comments will proceed from the state of my own memory, which is one of basically not remembering. My lack of memory here is quite strange considering the vivid visual images that I have retained of Foucault behind the lectern when he spoke about Manet at the Maison Franco-Japonaise in 1970. Foucault's mannerisms in front of images of Manet paintings projected on the screen, as he pointed to details with a long stick that he snapped like a whip, made a vivid impression, to the point that people watched captivated from every corner of the room—even if I myself experienced a kind of misgiving. At the beginning of his conversation with Ryūmei (Takaaki) Yoshimoto, "*Méthodologie pour la connaissance du monde: comment se débarrasser du marxisme*" (*Dits et écrits III*, p. 594), Foucault mentions that I had given him a rundown of Yoshimoto's work, but I have no memory of when, where, or in what form I might have had such a meeting with Foucault.

The only thing that I do remember is when I went with Foucault by taxi to a café that a Canadian staying with Maurice Pinguet was running in one of the old commercial areas of Tokyo. I don't remember why we had to go there in particular, but I do recall a relaxed Foucault taking in the stylish interior and saying to the Canadian proprietor, "this should become a hub for the transmission of French culture to Japan". I confess to having found it a little strange to hear Foucault speak this sentence, which sounded like something a cultural bureaucrat might say. Of course, as a young man Foucault had held a position in Sweden not unlike that of Maurice Pinguet in his own role as director of the Institut Franco-Japonais, which probably explains this comment.

I leave it to you to decide whether the foregoing observations were a necessary detour. Now I would like to turn to what you have in mind when you say that *La volonté de savoir* constituted "something like a 'crisis' in Foucault's own work". As I've already mentioned, when I bought this book and gave it a fast read in preparation for the interview, following just the thread of the argument, I did experience a kind of misgiving. To continue with the metaphor from above, my misgiving was probably a feeling of shock, of a kind, at the way that Foucault suddenly seemed to have given up being an absolutely "wise monkey" to become a relatively "wise human". Perhaps this happened under the influence of his Collège de France colleague, the historian of ancient Rome Paul Veyne (himself no ordinary "human"), but it seemed to me as if he had returned to being just a mediocre individual, living in Europe under the shared belief of a self with ancient Greece and Rome as origin sites in matters of both thought and sensibility. I sensed a dilution of the fictionality, and its corresponding textual reality, that of necessity runs through circumstances that developed in France—madness, incarceration, epistemic shifts, and so on. Here I find myself going back to Maurice Blanchot: "Even Foucault eventually returned to Greece ..." (*Michel Foucault, tel que je l'imagine*, 1986). I also did not think that this new book was "historical" in the true Foucauldian sense despite having the word "history" in the title. I found it surprisingly thin in its attachment to the "now (present)" as starting point for narrating this history.

Still, I did believe that describing problems surrounding "sexual phenomena" was a necessary if also enormous detour taken by Foucault in order to return to the "now (present)". In this regard, I find it deeply regretful that Foucault had to pass without having had the opportunity fully to realize this return.

9. Foucault was interested not simply in the translation and discussion of his own work, but also in carrying on a discussion with Japanese intellectuals, notably, with Masao Maruyama and Ryumei Yoshimoto. The French Embassy has kept many additional materials regarding Foucault's relations with them, as well as about his other related activities or initiatives during his trip. Looking back, how do you see this side of Foucault's Lectures?

This is a somewhat complex subject. I think that what I have to say will be important for understanding the Masao Maruyama of that point in time. The political struggles that took place on college campuses between 1968 and 1969 drove Maruyama from his position as a leading intellectual and transformed his image into that of a "person of the past". To use your language, he was no longer seen as a "political intellectual", having been ousted from the forefront of intellectual life in Japan. I do not know how aware Foucault would have been of these circumstances. In any case, Maruyama took actions that amounted to willful opposition, as a contemporary, to developments that were taking place simultaneously in various parts of the world from 1968 to 1969, so I will first explain the circumstances during this time period.

In January of 1969, the University of Tokyo's Yasuda Hall was occupied by a faction of the New Left (members of the "Zenkyōtō" All-Campus Joint Struggle League, a student group that had staged a backlash against the Japanese Communist Party). Yasuda Hall was "liberated" through the intervention of police force, but things only grew more complex after this incident. During a strike by students in each of the University of Tokyo's academic divisions, classrooms as well as offices in the Faculty of Law where Maruyama was appointed were violently occupied, and for a time classes showed no prospect of resuming. In the midst of this disorder, statements that Maruyama made while debates among the students were ongoing only worsened matters. Entering the main gate of the Hongō campus and heading straight toward Yasuda Hall, the classrooms and offices of the Faculty of Law extend to the right, facing an iconic ginkgo tree–lined path. The buildings are representative within the scenery of the University of Tokyo. For Maruyama, the occupation of these structures by students reflected inexcusably uncivilized behavior. He was quoted, responding in some daily newspaper, as saying: "Even the militarists did not do this kind of thing, not even the Nazis, such rioting". What he meant by "militarists" here was of course Japan's military leadership during the Second World War, their oppressive and unreasonable behavior.

As Maruyama's statement became broadly known, he became the target of severe criticism from all directions, starting with Ryūmei

(Takaaki) Yoshimoto and of course the New Left activists, but also extending to the general public. It is not as if there was no understanding out there for what he wanted to express. But his foolishly chosen words, claiming that the New Left movement in Japan was far more uncivilized between 1968 and 1969 than the aggressions of Germany's Third Reich and Japan's militarists, actors that had plunged the world into chaos, created the impression that he had forfeited his position as a leading intellectual. I myself recall being astonished by the crudeness of his metaphor, one that sought the appearance of basis in human history but actually misjudged its reality. In fact, even during the Second World War, university leadership had denied campus intrusions by police forces. The problem with the university administration abandoning this kind of policy of its own initiative and welcoming riot police on campus grounds, was in part a matter of a sudden change in the university itself, and students were victims of that change of approach. By deriding the response of those in the position of the victim, Maruyama abdicated, of his own accord, his rights and responsibilities to contribute as a concerned party to the international developments underway between 1968 and 1969.

Reaching, for purposes of comparison, to the violence of imperial Japan's militarists, or to the brutality of the Third Reich, violence and brutality that defy human understanding, amounted to an extraordinarily mediocre insistence, one that might qualify for classification in an updated 20th- to 21st-century edition of Gustave Flaubert's *Dictionnaire des idées reçues* under the entry of "postmodernism", alongside the language that those on either side of the present war in Ukraine often use to denounce one another—a way of thinking utterly detached from reality. This way of thinking takes the Nazi period for one in which everyone involved identified with the same way of thinking, an incoherent perspective that pretends as if no assassination attempt had been made against Hitler. The same is true with respect to imperial Japan, where we can cite one very "liberal", if not anti-war, incident, for example, that took place in the capital city Tokyo. The date was probably sometime in the latter part of 1944 when the American aerial bombing of Tokyo had intensified. In Room 25 of the Faculty of Law facilities, the largest lecture hall at the University of Tokyo, a screening for students of *Gone with the Wind* (1939, Victor Fleming) was held, using a print that had probably been confiscated by the Japanese military forces in Singapore. Despite the fact that this would have been the first screening of this technicolor Hollywood film in Japan, and therefore an historic event, all traces of its having happened have been expunged even from the records in the Faculty of Law, and as a result this has become an incident shrouded in mystery. When I was president of the University of Tokyo, I searched to the best of my ability for evidence, but this episode remains a riddle to this day. The witnesses who have testified to having attended this screening were mostly graduates of the medical and engineering programs. I never found a law graduate who claimed to have been in attendance. The reason for this is probably because most students in the liberal arts had been enlisted in domestic wartime mobilization duties in 1944, leaving only those in the science and technology fields behind on campus. In any case, Dr. Reona Ezaki, who was awarded a Nobel Prize in physics in 1973, testifies to having taken part in this event and having been present for the screening. He attests that the second part of the screening was interrupted by an intensified air raid, so this is probably something that actually took place. He also claims that most of the students who saw the film were of the opinion that there was no winning a war against a country that produced such a thing. Maruyama's statement—"Even the militarists did not do this kind of thing, not even the Nazis, such rioting"—entirely excludes consideration of such kinds of circumstances and seeks to paint that period in black and white, in abstract terms. The event of this screening of *Gone with the Wind* in Room 25 at the University of Tokyo in the late stages of the Second World War attests to the fact that, even under the militarist regime in imperial Japan, there were not a few people of a "liberal" orientation who, if not exactly anti-war, at least sought to stem the worsening of conditions. This is one sense in which Maruyama's statement merits an entry in the *Dictionnaire des idées reçues*.

At the time, I had not yet been appointed to my teaching position at the University of Tokyo and was working at a certain private university in Tokyo, but I was an observer of the tactics of the All-Campus Joint Struggle League movement and did not necessarily approve of what I saw. Still, I was conscious of the fact that talking through things with the students occupying classrooms was the duty of a faculty member, even a privilege, and I personally worked to persuade student activists through all-night discussions, advocating for the resumption of classes, something that they accepted. Maruyama was of course approaching his late 50s, and his age limited him here in some ways, but to cut off conversation with the students—with a statement like "Even the militarists did not do this kind of thing, not even the Nazis, such rioting"—and for a professor of political thought to speak so erratically, gave the impression of someone retreating emptily into a false authority. Indeed, he ended up not being able to withstand the probing of the students and fell ill. He was hospitalized and went into retirement from his duties at the University of Tokyo earlier than he otherwise should have.

This background is enough to demonstrate that Masao Maruyama adopted precisely the opposite attitude as Michel Foucault did in his own relationship to the, in a sense, "New Left" young activists in Paris of 1968. I do not know the first thing about when and where Foucault and Maruyama met in 1978, about what kind of a meeting it was, or what they discussed. I also do not know how aware Foucault may or may not have been about this embarrassing history of his interlocutor. In any case, it is not hard to imagine that Foucault was unusually at ease in the free and open English conversation he had with Maruyama, much like in his unrestrained English conversations with students and faculty at Berkeley, or later at Columbia and other universities in the American Northeast. His other public conversations in Japan during this period were mostly facilitated by an interpreter, as, for example, in the case of his conversation with Ichio Asukata, who was at the time Chairman of the Japan Socialist Party. The idea of inviting Maruyama to the Collège de France was probably a product of the open atmosphere of such unmediated dialogue. Still, if Foucault had had even some background knowledge about the Faculty of Law at the University of Tokyo, it would not have been surprising if he had reached out to professor of law Noriyuki Noda, who had already had an opportunity to give a lecture at the University of Paris and had published a book called *Introduction au droit japonais* (Dalloz, 1966), for example.

From my perspective, it was a much greater honor to be a colleague of Noriyuki Noda than of Maruyama. This relates to how much I disdained Maruyama's book *Nihon no shisō* (*Japanese Thought*), which was published when I was a graduate student at the University of Tokyo. This book about "Japanese thought", which was oblivious to the obvious fact that it was itself an example of "Japanese thought", ended up discussing what it took for "Japanese thought" in very abstract terms. The introduction to the chapter called "Japanese Thought" near the beginning of the book includes the following text: "The problem lies in the fact that I *myself* know the nature of Japan's 'modernity', which uniquely combines *super-modernity* and *pre-modernity*" (p. 5). Just who wrote this book? Is it because he alone was exempted from the nature of "Japan's 'modernity'"—its "unique fusion" of "*super-modernity*" and "*pre-modernity*"—that the Maruyama who wrote these words was so rightfully positioned to treat this modernity as an object of narration? Or perhaps this itself is the essence of what you call a "particular co-existence" of Japanese with European "modernity".

10. How then do you explain Foucault's attitude to Maruyama?

As you suggest, Foucault's sympathy for the political movement against the construction of Narita airport at the time, is very legitimate. In Japan, this movement is called the "Sanrizuka Struggle" after the Sanrizuka area in Chiba Prefecture where construction of the new airport had been planned. A 1967 government decision was at the origin of this struggle, and the movement opposing the airport became inseparably related to the 1968–69 struggles on university campuses. Farmers and workers took part alongside students in this event, which even now has not reached a conclusion—a movement that can be called one of the significant events of Japan's postwar period. Maruyama maintained silence on this topic. Working from the unique position of treating the "movement" itself as an exercise in "filming", the great filmmaker

Shinsuke Ogawa, by contrast, made a series of rousing documentaries in this space, starting with *Summer in Narita* (1968), documentaries that gave shape to an important state of affairs, one in which the social movements of 1968–69 in Japan were accompanied by cinema, indicating the breadth of their reach. I don't know if Foucault ever saw Ogawa's films, but I would like you to see them, if you have not, as someone with more than a passing interest in the Japan of this period.

With respect to Maruyama's books, the ones that are still widely read today include the problematic *Japanese Thought*, of course, but also his first book, *Studies in the Intellectual History of Tokugawa Japan* (*Nihon seiji shisō-shi kenkyū*, 1952, reissued 1983). I do think that his critical decoding of Edo-period Confucian tradition is comparatively well done. He strikes just the right tone in describing a past like that of the Tokugawa period. Still, I myself am quite skeptical about whether this tradition functioned as the source of imperialism in Japan. The reason for my skepticism is because he fails to demonstrate self-awareness in his methods when thinking about the "present tense" or the "present era" of thought. While studies concerning Maruyama have continued to be written, I do also have substantial questions about whether these have really demonstrated novel readings of his work. In any case, I personally do not want to think that the Maruyama described here had any significant influence on Foucault. I also do not want to think of Foucault as someone shallow enough to have been influenced by a thinker without having undertaken a detailed reading of his writings. Needless to say, all of this is just a matter of personal will.

11. *How do you see the discussion of Zen in the Lectures in relation to "Western" views?*

As for the interest that Western intellectuals have taken in "Zen", there is something here that I find hard fully to understand. The most important problem in Japan today lies in the "emperor system", something with which the country has not been able to part. The "emperor system" lacks the kind of visual attractive force of "Zen"—the costuming of monks, the formal architecture of temples, the gardens, and so on—and intellectuals, starting with but not limited to Maruyama, have mostly avoided confronting the fact that the nation of Japan remains an "imperial" power, and the incontestable fact that Shinto, not Zen, is at the core of its "emperor system", despite the fact that questions of how to deal with such matters are in fact the real issue. From my elementary to high school years, I attended a school that children of the imperial family also attended. The boy who would become emperor had the nickname "Brown Pig"—his friends called him this because he looked like a well fattened pig in swim class[6]—indicating how little respect we had for the imperial institution. And yet, a vague sense of veneration for this person who has now stepped down and become "emperor emeritus" is widely present in the Japan of today. Whether intentionally or unconsciously, people tend to refuse taking up the bothersome problem of the "control that is not control" of the "emperor system" when thinking about the problems of contemporary Japan. The left has even ended up in the inverted position, if anything, of supporting the present emperor, since he has argued for thorough adherence to the constitution and against the position of the present government that favors revising the constitution to allow Japan to maintain a standing military. Unfortunately, Foucault never focused his sights on this "emperor system", the invisible power structure to which contemporary Japan is subject. Perhaps it was Roland Barthes who most clearly perceived the situation when, in *Empire des signes*, he described the Imperial Palace—residence of the emperor—as occupying the center of Tokyo, but as an absence, an empty center.

12. *Yoshimoto went on to write a long letter to Foucault in praise of his published exchange with Zen monks. What was your relationship with him?*

As I've already mentioned, Yoshimoto was exemplary as a leading intellectual during the university campus struggles from 1968 to 1969, standing on the side of the students and stimulating them. He also drew a clear line between this and Japan Communist Party–affiliated movements. I do not know to what extent he was a deep reader of Marx. I was present for his conversation with Foucault and assisted the two of them with simultaneous interpretation, but honestly, I never understood along the way how they were perceiving each other, whether their expressions of sympathy toward each other were merely formal or sincere. This remained the case even after I read R. Nakamura's French translation of the recording of this conversation published in *Dits et écrits*.

Yoshimoto, who was also a poet, had attracted an established readership with texts that could be called theoretical, such as *Gengo ni totte bi to wa nani ka* (*What is Beauty for Language?*, Keisō Shobō, 1963) or *Kyōdō gensō-ron* (*The Collective Illusion*, Kawade Shobō Shinsha, 1968), but he was also a literary critic. In this capacity, I was fortunate to have multiple opportunities to meet him, and I also took part in a conversation with him for the literary magazine *Umi*. Still, we never once shared a common point of view. As a literary critic, he took the position that all great works were "tragedies". In my view this looked like little more than a poor "romanticism". From the mid-1980s, he was seen as having converted to so-called postmodernism, through books like *Masu imēji-ron* (*The Mass Image*, Fukutake Shoten, 1984), but even during this time he would say that those who had never read *Les mots et les choses* were "unqualified", so Yoshimoto seems never to have lost his respect for the Foucault of at least a certain period.

In thinking about the problem of power in Japan, it is not "Zen" but "Shinto"—which lies behind the "emperor system"—that demands reflection. I myself have also not written about this topic directly. In fact, there is no one in contemporary Japan who has seriously taken on this subject. I have only made indirect reference to it. This was in my as yet untranslated article "'Reigai' no reigaiteki na yōgo: Ozu Yasujirō Tokyo monogatari-ron", *Bungaku* 9, no. 2 (March 26, 2008): 178. For the most part, we find neither *kamidana* (Shinto) nor *butsudan* (Buddhist) household shrines or altars in the Japanese houses that Ozu depicted. Ozu's own grave is in fact located in a Zen temple in Kamakura. But this is not because he believed in Zen. In deliberately excluding household shrines and altars from his sets, he also indirectly swept the "emperor system" from the field of view. The character for "nothingness" (mu) inscribed on his gravestone is not Buddhist in the least. "Nothingness" in Ozu is literally the empty space that he arrived at in eliminating both shrines and altars.

Translated by Ryan Cook

NOTES

1 Maurice Pinguet (1929–1991) is perhaps best known in English for his work with Roland Barthes on *The Empire of Signs*, and his own magisterial study of *Voluntary Death in Japan*, published in French in 1984, translated into English shortly after. But he also maintained relations with Foucault going back to their student years together at the Ecole Normal Supérieure. In 1985, shortly after Foucault's own untimely death, Pinguet published in Japanese a striking portrait looking back at Foucault's formative years, translated into French a year later. It can now be found together with additional materials in Maurice Pinguet, *Le texte Japon*, ed. Michel Ferrier, Seuil, 2009.

2 *Magazine Littéraire*, no 325, Octobre 1994, pp. 24ff.

3 Maruyama had prepared a detailed history of the role of "political intellectuals" in Japan, set in Asia, and going back to the Tokugawa Shogunate. Yoshimoto wrote a long letter in praise of Foucault's exchange with Zen monks, and the ways it served as an antidote to the prevailing "Western" views about Zen. The holdings at IMEC also detail Foucault's many activities, his visit to prisons, his participation in a demonstration at an airport, and his correspondence with various political figures. An inventory can be found in (https://www.imec-archives.com/); they can be consulted in person.

4 *Shisō* and *shikō* are related words that can both be translated as "thought" or "thinking", with the distinction that *shisō* indicates a higher level of processing or abstraction, related to thinking within systems of thought or ideologies as opposed to from direct experience [Translator's note].

5 The word *michi* is a noun, used, for example, in the Japanese translation of Plato's famous phrase, "I know that I know nothing". [Translator's note.]

6 It has also been speculated that the young Prince Akihito was given this name because his dark skin tone resembled the brown glaze on common pig-shaped ceramic containers for anti-mosquito incense coils. [Translator's note.]

INDEX